The Art of Living
in
SINGAPORE

Nicoline Lopez
Coordinator and Designer

▲

Gérald Lopez
Photographer

▲

Manon Lopez
Writer and Assistant Designer

NGM PUBLISHERS
SOUTH EAST ASIA

Dedicated to our very special friend

Henry de Saint-Laon

The Art of Living in Singapore

Published in 1994 by
NGM Publishers
SOUTH EAST ASIA

First Edition
ISBN No : 981-00-5490-4

Enquiries should be directed to
NGM Publishers
20A Jalan Mamanda 5, Ampang Point,
68000 Selangor, Malaysia   Fax : (603) 451 7079
or
Thong Teck Building, 15 Scotts Road, #04 - 01/03
Singapore 0922   Fax : (65) 733 5497

Edited by
Barbara Dare

Colour Separation by	Artwork and Typesetting by	Printed and Bound by
Colourscan	Elaine Cheong	Tien Wah Press (Pte) Ltd
Singapore	Kuala Lumpur	Singapore

acknowledgements

We would like to express our indebtedness and profound gratitude to a very dear friend, Henry de Saint-Laon, and to two other friends who wish to remain anonymous, for their benevolent generosity and faith in us; for without them this book would not have been possible.

This publication has certainly been a challenging project but a most pleasurable effort thanks to the kind co-operation and support of the home owners : Mr. and Mrs. Chollet, Mr. and Mrs. Bongi, Dr. and Mrs. Lee Suan Yew, Joseph Lam, Mr. and Mrs. Davies, Pierre and Chantal Gourragne, Mr. and Mrs. Tomlin, Bruno and Soraya Stackler, Amanda Richardson, Mr. and Mrs. Chan Soo Khian, Mr. and Mrs. Mark Tan, Frank Marciano and Robin Goh, Christian and Martine de Saint Hilaire, Mr. and Dr. Selvadurai, Bill Shepherd and Jim Bowen, Mr. and Mrs. Pellegrin, Dr. and Mrs. Chan Ah Kow, Mr. and Mrs. de Montferrand, and the other home owners who do not wish to be mentioned by name. Our thanks also to Mr. Tan Swie Hian, the Goodwood, Duxton and Regent hotels, Alkaff Mansion and Kinara Restaurant.

We are deeply grateful to Dr. David Marshall, who has done us the great honour of writing the preface. We would like to extend our thanks to all those who have given us their encouragement and spontaneous assistance; Marika Clarke, Francois de Grancey, Dr. Masood Faizullah, Puan Sri Eileen Kuok, David Mun, Nan Sandford, Yuen Yim Theng, Jan Bell, and to special friends, Chantal Gourragne and Arlette Rajalingam. To the professionals who have given us their invaluable advice and services, we would like to express our sincere appreciation, especially to Barbara Dare, our editor, whose skill and efficiency has been an indispensable asset to the realisation of this book; and Elaine Cheong for all her patient endeavours in assisting us in making the presentation of " The Art of Living in Singapore" distinctive.

 The special seal signifies unique lifestyles in Singapore

 The endless knot symbolises long life uninterrupted by setbacks

 The clouds are auspicious harbingers of peace and happiness

preface

" IN THE WORLD, A HOME;
IN THE HOME, YOUR WORLD "
(Goethe)

The art of interior decoration is the art of creating your own world within the world.

In seeking to express our personality in our ambiance, we often lack knowledge of materials and forms available. It is in this sphere that we are indebted to the experienced eye and aesthetic feel of Nicoline Lopez and her talented family team. They have portrayed extensive examples of many beautiful homes in Singapore as well as selected hotels, restaurants and even a private museum; over three hundred and fifty illustrations reveal outstanding talent for exquisite and sometimes stunning reproduction of homes and scenes.

By way of bonus, we have a brief history of Singapore, its people and the multi-faceted facilities of gracious living. This is a book that should not only grace coffee-tables but should also be a reference in the art of living and an excellent souvenir for foreigners. My respects to Nicoline, Gérald and Manon, who though based in Kuala Lumpur, have contributed materially to Singapore's cultural scene and my thanks to them for a pleasant new vision of some aspects of our country.

DAVID MARSHALL

The Art of Living
in
SINGAPORE

"The Art of Living in Singapore" offers a glimpse into homes which would otherwise remain strictly private. The featured interiors have been decorated by Singaporeans or by those who have made their home in the region for many years and were selected by virtue of the fact that they displayed a profound awareness of regional cultures, combined with a unique, original and, naturally, personal perspective. The result is a valuable contribution to the stimulation of new ideas in Singaporean interior design and decor.

Interest in this lively, lovely style shows no bounds as increasing awareness in European and American markets leads to Asian materials being used more and more in conjunction with Western decors. Exciting trends have married age-old treasures with brilliant oriental fabrics; antiques from Penang and Malacca, and as far afield as Vietnam and China with prints and tapestries from Russia and France.

The beautiful pages of this book show by clear example that attractive and sophisticated interiors are not necessarily achieved through huge expenditure. Bold, imaginative use of what is available locally can make a budget seem as if it were unbounded, can transform the mundane to the miraculous.

GEOGRAPHICAL AND HISTORICAL SETTING

A brief history of Singapore outlining its importance as a trading and strategic port, the various cultural influences and modern-day aspects to life in this forward-thinking city.

HOME INTERIORS

This, the major segment of the book, illustrates styles of living from colonial houses, including an existing rubber planter's home, to high-tech interiors situated in ultra-modern condominiums.

PUBLIC AND COMMERCIAL INTERIORS

A unique museum, three hotels chosen for their individual decor, and two captivating restaurants.

ARCHITECTURE OF SINGAPORE

Everyday street scenes illustrate the tremendous diversity which has developed over the decades. Prominent buildings, old and new, make up this backdrop, from new banking headquarters to traditional temples tenaciously clinging to their original sites.

SOURCES FOR REFERENCE

The book closes with "The Art of Shopping" - selected names and addresses of speciality shops for the home, interior designers and decorators and restaurants for enjoyment.

Singapore

Island of Orchids

The Republic of Singapore consists of a main island some 42 kilometres in length and 23 kilometres in breadth, together with a scattering of small islands, located approximately 136 kilometres north of the equator. A causeway, just over 1,000 metres long, links Singapore to the Malaysian Peninsula to the north, while the Indonesian archipelago lies immediately to the south.

In January 1819, Sir Thomas Stamford Raffles established a settlement, a trading post for the English East India Company, on what was then a sparsely populated island at the southern end of the Straits of Malacca. In 1867 the Straits Settlements became a Crown Colony and Singapore was, for more than 100 years, one of the most prosperous ports not just of British Malaya but in the entire British Empire. Prosperity, as trade expanded in the 1860's prompted the population to swell to in excess of 80,000 - over 60% of whom were Chinese; Tamil immigrants also arrived, brought in for labour and artisan skills.

Singapore's strategic position had been noted for many centuries. A third-century Chinese account described it as *Pu-luo-chung* or island at the end of a peninsula. Chinese travellers and Portuguese historians, within Malay Annals and Javanese histories, refer to Singapore and it featured in the Javanese *Nagarakretagama* of 1365 as *Temasek* or *Sea Town.* An eyewitness report, also dating from the 14th century, was provided by Wang Ta-Yuan, a Chinese trader who describes the *"Dragon Teeth Gate",* believed to have been the western entrance to the present-day Keppel Harbour. He told of a settlement of traders and also pirates who preyed upon Chinese junks passing through the Straits.

Ownership passed between Siamese and Java-based empires until the latter part of the 14th century when it became part of the new Malay kingdom of Malacca and the name *Singapura, Lion City,* was first used. Following the fall of Malacca to the Portuguese in 1511, Singapore became an outpost for the Malacca Sultanate which took refuge along the estuary of the Johore River until, in 1587, the Portuguese destroyed Johore Lama. In 1641 the Portuguese themselves were displaced by the Dutch whose colonies had flourished in Java and the Spice Islands. In 1786 the British influence spread with their acquisition of Penang, in 1819 they secured Singapore and in 1824 the Dutch transferred their rights over Malacca to the British. When Raffles arrived, the Malays held political power under the control of the Temenggong, one of the two principal ministers of the Johore-Riau Sultanate.

The earliest entrepôt trade of Singapore included coarse gold, Chinese porcelain, iron cooking utensils, blue satin and cotton prints. The Straits of Malacca saw vast movement of goods between China, Siam, Cambodia and Vietnam in the east and the Indian subcontinent, Arabia and Persia to the west, as well as markets in Europe. Command of the sea was crucial and Singapore, with its natural deep water anchorage, was well placed for the Bugis traders, Chinese junks and western sailing ships.

In 1819, however, all the early British settlers found was a fishing village, a coastal environment which was largely swampy, traces of well established fruit groves inland and some Chinese farmers producing gambier. At first, the main anchorage of the sailing vessels was Boat Quay. Then, emphasising the importance of Singapore with its free port status at the crossroads between the Indian and Pacific Oceans, came the development of Keppel Harbour. In 1913 the Singapore Harbour Board was formed to run all the Port services.

Private enterprise expanded at a phenomenal rate with Raffles Place becoming a trading centre for western companies and banks. In 1870, telegraphic communication revolutionised trade with the industrial nations. Singapore became an attractive focal point for British commercial investment and Chinese immigration. The growth of tin mining and, later, the rubber-planting industries provoked further growth. The advent of steamships, together with opening of the Suez Canal, also helped enormously. Singapore became an essential link.

The 122 year period of uninterrupted peace came to a halt when Singapore fell to the Japanese on 15 February 1942. The formal surrender of the Japanese in Singapore at the close of World War II took place on 12 September 1945. The war years made a deep impression on those who, a generation later, pressed for self government. Lee Kuan Yew, a lawyer, (Prime Minister 1959 to 1990) gradually gained influence, political power, respect and support. He inaugurated the People's Action Party (PAP) in November 1954 which became a major political entity. In 1959 the PAP swept the polls. On 16 September 1963, Singapore, Sabah and Sarawak united with Malaya to form Malaysia but fears of Singapore being unable to retain its identity and its rights were among the reasons that led to Singapore separating from Malaysia within two years and becoming an independent sovereign state on 9 August 1965.

Membership of a five power alliance with the United Kingdom, Australia, New Zealand and Malaysia contributed to national security. The infrastructure was strengthened across the island. The Economic Development Board was established in 1961 to invest in new industries and new industrial sites and to accelerate the growth of existing ones. Activities increased in the financial sector and there was a dramatic economic transformation.

During the 1970's and 1980's trade was supplemented by remarkable development in manufacturing, transport and communications, banking and finance, and tourism. Foreign investment was sought and Singapore evolved into an international financial centre offering a wide range of services and sophisticated facilities, including the latest in telecommunications. A high emphasis was put on education, further education, strong forward-thinking leadership and the role of ASEAN, (Association of South East Asian Nations).

With the swift modernisation, inevitably sights of old Singapore began to disappear. Sunrise and sunset outline the startling silhouette of a progressive city couched amongst the architecture of earlier times. Although the old buildings often become dilapidated, they possess a special grace and a great sense of history pervades almost every street corner. In 1983 a Master Plan for conservation was unveiled and the relentless construction that is a hallmark of modern Singapore became better balanced with preservation and restoration. Historic buildings continue to chronicle the past, from 19th century temples to the Cathay Building, Singapore's first high-rise building, standing at 16-storeys. It contained the Cathay Cinema which opened in October 1939 and was the first public space to be air-conditioned.

The cultural diversity of Chinese, Malay, Indian, Peranakan (Straits Chinese) and European races continues to intertwine and enrich the fabric of Singapore. A magical aspect to this country is therefore this exotic fusion: familiar well-patronised corner coffee houses, Arab alleyways, Chinatown shophouses fronted by five-foot-ways, street barbers and medicine shops, Indian garland stalls and spice merchants, back-street batik printers and crouching cobblers. Glimpses that turn the clock back may only be a few steps away from some of the world's most outstanding hotels and extensive, inviting, shopping plazas.

Traditional observances continue in temples amongst incense and Chinese deities, guarded by dramatic dragons and Door Gods; *Bilals* proclaim the hours of prayer from the cool dignity of the mosques; dramatic images flaunted from temple rooftops beckon Hindus to their colourful celebrations and observances; the quiet corners of Christian worship include the Armenian Church built in 1835 and the glistening sanctuary of St Andrew's Cathedral, consecrated in 1862.

The majority of Singaporeans now live on pristine housing estates, in apartments with every amenity. The public housing, known as HDB (Housing Development Board, established in1960) provides apartment homes for some 87% of the almost three million population. Some of these apartments are situated on reclaimed land, most include recreational and sports facilities. So impressive have been these efforts that the Tampines town project won the World Habitat Award of 1992, a United Nations' housing award. Entered for the Developing Country Category, it was upgraded by judges to the Developed Country Category.

Expatriates find Singapore a very pleasant place to live, with its high standards of cleanliness, medical facilities, superb services such as Changi Airport and the MRT subway. Impressions of modern Singapore also confirm the description *"Garden City"*, as the island provides a showcase for some of the world's finest orchids. These include the national flower, *Vanda Miss Joaquim,* as well as many vivid examples of tropical plants such as Heliconia, and the vivid Bougainvillaea which cascades from bridges and balconies. The environment is drastically different from the early days of crocodiles and tigers, undrained swamps and buffaloes lumbering beside canals. The efficient urban ambience that has been created amid the unique variety of cultures contributes to the distinctive lifestyle that can be enjoyed in Singapore today.

Where Singapore began.
A view of the Padang and Boat Quay.

Unpretentious, informal and friendly are some of the adjectives Dolores Chollet uses to describe the Lion City. The Chollets first became acquainted with Singapore fourteen years ago when Mr.Chollet served as the French Ambassador. Upon his retirement from the diplomatic service, they returned to settle.

Being an outdoor person, Dolores Chollet greatly enjoys the opportunities Singapore offers. When she has time to spare, between her busy schedule as an interior designer she pursues one particular activity with diligent enthusiasm - horse riding - and her treasures at home include equestrian trophies and a collection of horses in all shapes, forms and sizes from around the world.

An illusion of space has been created in the sunken sitting-room with the extensive and elegant use of glass and mirrors and with Perspex stands and shelves. Although the flavour is European, the works of art from Asia, South America and the Caribbean are given their own careful place which lets them contribute their special appeal to the lively atmosphere. The sitting and dining-rooms open on to long, narrow terraces which allow for the display of plants and for light; to Dolores Chollet, both are important aspects of life in Singapore.

A flying, antique, wooden horse with stylised cloud detail, bearing an arrangement of white lilies and orchids. The silver flower in the foreground is from Portugal. The petals on this ingenious flower can be detached, inverted and used as ashtrays.

Left : The unadorned glass sliding doors keep the dining-room bright. The mural carvings from Haiti are made from metal oil drums and the large one represents a market scene. On the sideboard is a fine spirit house from Thailand. The wrought-iron standing candelabrum is from Sri Lanka.

Below : The exotic master bedroom with a striking zebra print bedcover. All the colourful naive paintings on the wall are Haitian.

Left : Full view of the sitting-room, the sliding glass doors open on to a terrace. In this light decor, full of animation, the collection of horses from around the world is prominent. The largest one is a wooden sculpture from India. Above it is an antique Peruvian sun mirror and on either side hang a pair of Mexican carvings. The blue head and the stone torso are replicas of pieces found in the Louvre. A portrait drawing by Picasso stands serene in the corner and Indian stone figures feature on Perspex stands, together with a papier-mâché, antique Buddha head from Burma.

Colours are very important in this home. They welcome you with pleasure and warmth and bring to life this striking interior of quintessential simplicity. Furnished and decorated with a variety of items from diverse origins, there prevails a harmony in substance and essence. Odile Bongi explains that her decor is basically an extension of her own personality. In addition she has tried to create her idea of a home in the tropics. "I used to dream about Singapore and what it would be like, but when I arrived it did not seem as oriental as I had expected. However, the longer you are here the more of the exotic aspects you absorb."

Built on sloping ground this "Black and White" bungalow stands on stilts, elevated as high as ten feet above the ground at the front. The void deck keeps the house cool and is put to good use, serving as a casual dining area and playroom for the children. The kitchen and servants' quarters are situated apart from the main house at the top of the slope, linked by a covered walkway. The black half timbering and white plaster resembles English Tudor architecture; the stilts, overhangs and verandahs are adapted from the Malay *kampong* house. This eclectic style of the 1920's and 30's adequately resolved the problems of the sweltering heat, yet provided a comforting reminder of home for British civil servants braving the tropics. In modern times, these bungalows continue to be much sought after for their nostalgic charm and open living. Exotic and appropriate, they are particularly special in Singapore where many old houses have been demolished to make way for new buildings and condominiums.

In an interior that seems to integrate so naturally with the flourishing flora outside, it is not surprising to find every room enlivened with arrangements of flowers and greenery.

Breakfast set for two in the cool shade of the deck beneath the house.
Against one pillar stands a Balinese goddess in sandstone. Hanging
on the other is a dainty wooden bird trap from Lombok, Indonesia.

Left : View of the sitting-room. The centre rattan sofa is flanked by two green, Chinese porcelain stools and a pair of teak, Burmese *nats* (temple angels) on lotus-shaped pedestals. Beyond, through the frame of the open windows, are the leaves of a Traveller's Palm, fanned out in almost perfect symmetry. In the corner of the room is a handsome, antique, red, lacquered, wedding cabinet from Northern China. Among the other lacquer-work is a Burmese offering tray in which are nestled three ostrich eggs from South Africa and a Burmese offering box, mounted into a lamp.

Top Right : A palm leaf and a few wild flowers brought together in a fluted glass vase. On the ground is a food cover and basket in very fine bamboo work.

Below : In the foreground, a hand-crafted grass duck from France and on the side table a Filipino rice basket made into a lamp. An Indian cotton dhurrie floor covering sets off the Perspex coffee table.

In the dining-room there is a glass-topped table with rattan chairs and against the wall stands a kitchen cabinet in Nakka wood from the Philippines. Displayed on the top of this is a Balinese offering tray and a sea coconut shell (*Coco de Mer*, found only in Seychelles). The two bird cages are part of a collection from around the world and the oil painting is typical of the vibrant, native works found in Bali.

Top : Exterior shot of the house and the garden which Odile Bongi spent many hours, indeed days, taming and landscaping when they first moved in three years ago.

Below Left : A pretty composition that sums up the refined simplicity of this interior. Above the "pineapple chair", inspired by a Creole design, hangs a beaded

Balinese food cover. Along the corridor is a wicker chaise longue from France and a fresh bouquet in a contemporary blue and white porcelain pot. Carrying his own load of orchids is a little terracotta turtle from Mexico.

Below Right : Exotic fruits and dinner plates with tropical motifs to match.

Left : The master bedroom with windows and French doors all around overlooking the verandahs. The wicker bedhead and side tables are from the Philippines and the various baskets are from India, Thailand and Indonesia. The tapestry on the wall is a modern piece from Brazil made of wool, silk and cotton threads, representing parrots and ducks, by Madeleine Colaco. The antique armchair is a French Voltaire.

Above : The guest bedroom, with white cane furniture and French cotton bedlinen. On the wall is a contemporary Chinese painting on rice paper, depicting a wedding boat with all the good luck symbols for a healthy, fruitful life.

Whichever way one turns, this house is the fruit of much endeavour and the coming together of ideas reconciling shelter with nature. When designing the house, the architect's task was to work around an internal courtyard two storeys high and forty metres long. The owners, Dr. and Mrs. Lee Suan Yew, wanted "a tropical house that captures the romance of the East, the night air and the lush surroundings. A house that fits rather than fights with its environment". Of course there were practical criteria to fulfil - it had to be very secure, have good cross ventilation and be mosquito and rain proof without the necessity of closing the windows.

Mrs. Lee is the development director of the Singapore Tourist Promotion Board (STPB). She has been actively involved in some of Singapore's conservation projects such as the Empress Place Museum and Raffles Hotel. Sensitive to her environment and full of inspiration, Mrs. Lee keenly supervised every stage of the design and construction of their home.

Moving from the ground floor to the upper floor, there is a transition from stone and marble to timber and polished parquet. The interior assembles several compositions, from the ceremonious, classic arrangement of the antique, Chinese, rosewood furniture to the informality of substantial bamboo sofas and loose cushions. The essence of the decor is Chinese, enhanced by wooden Ming design grills, see-through glazed tiles and the pools (water and carp are significant in Chinese symbolism), with other Asian elements pleasantly blended in. In Mrs. Lee's words, "art is in the harmony" and her main aim has been to create a different ambience in each room, depending upon its function, whilst maintaining a continuity throughout.

Stairway leading to the first floor bedrooms and family room.

A view of the two storey atrium and the pool, the focal concept of the interior design. The specially constructed roof above opens the house to the outside elements and welcomes rain or shine. The black slate pools, flickering with the darting movements of the red and golden carp, serve to link yet separate the space, creating an exotic and significant setting.

House entrance with the fan shaped porch, inspired by a picture of a pavilion in Beijing's Summer Palace. The fan shape in Chinese feng-shui ensures that any good fortune that comes to the house will grow, like flames urged by the wind.

To enjoy the best effect of the pictures of this house one needs
to retain the harmony of the exterior photograph overleaf.

Top Left and left : One is greeted at the entrance passageway by Ng Eng Teng's bronze fondu sculpture of Sherlyn Lee (daughter of Dr. & Mrs. Lee), commissioned when she was five. She sits, pensively, in a traditional Chinese setting upon a rosewood bench. Behind is an ebony and glass screen. The graceful lotus are symbolic, attributed with purity and love.

Top Right : A conventional Chinese arrangement of a pair of carved, antique rosewood chairs and a high table, customarily used for tea ceremonies. Above, presides the portrait of a Lee ancestor from China.

19

View of a formal sitting area by the indoor pools. Beside the sofa is a
Straits Chinese, ceremonial, candlestick in red lacquer and gold leaf.

On the table, a very fine pair of ancient Chinese incense burners in pewter, intricately decorated and inlaid with stones and enamel. On the left is a collection of delicate jade pieces. The noteworthy lacquer painting is of the Lee ancestral home in China.

Above : A pair of Tang, ceramic, young ladies with a bird, standing under a bonsai tree.

Right : One of the informal seating areas furnished with the popular creations of a Filipino designer, famous for his elementary low-lying furniture. The open plan invites you to spend a quiet moment by the pool. The greenery of the garden outside is discreetly visible through the floral, etched glass-panelled windows.

The family room upstairs with a balcony to the right overlooking the atrium. The Ming-design timber grilled windows reveal the abundant greenery outside, true to the desired concept of a "tropical house". The gilded Burmese musicians' circle (the musicians were seated inside) converts into a stunning glass-topped table on which are placed an assortment of tidbits in jars and a wooden Nyonya jewellery case. The large sofas are covered with Indonesian blue and white ikat blankets which add warmth and informality to the room.

Left : Graceful, Chinese, antique set of rosewood table and stools, the table top inlaid with marble. On it is an exquisitely carved antique stand, presumably made to display precious ornaments.

Right : Displayed on the stand are two jade pendants resting on another delicate miniature stand. In a cloisonné bowl, an arrangement of wild fruit, cactus flowers and wild grass.

A glimpse into one of the daughters' rooms. The unusual wooden shutters along the walls permit the amount of daylight coming into the room to be controlled. A single bed is placed in a corner at an angle. A large cushion in striking brown and white batik lies on the floor while a teddy bear sits shyly on a simple cane chair.

On the marble-top table in the dining-room is a bouquet of lilies, pink orchids, leucadendrons and leaves from the garden arranged in a highly decorated, antique Chinese pot. The bunch of fresh lychee completes the exotic arrangement.

Joseph Lam is as exceptionally busy as are most top executives in the advertising world. His home is his lair; comfortable, manageable and filled with an "ethnic mish-mash" - as he puts it - of artifacts and antiques. He is strongly attracted to the Art Deco period and places his finds in no planned scheme but, rather, intuitively where he feels the most comfortable with them.

The high ceilings, rich *chengal* floor boards, Art Deco details - such as the ventilation diamonds - and the enveloping greenery outside, contribute a great deal to the relaxing, balmy atmosphere whilst the theme of the decor, masculine and sensitive, agreeably echoes the style of this single storey house. Beyond the lounge is the dining-room, served by a narrow, compact kitchen to the rear. Furnished with a solid teak table and handsome high back chairs, it is treated to a touch of drama in the evenings when dinner is set and the large candelabra are lit.

The bungalow is presumed to have been built in the 1920's or 30's and is one of three similar buildings on a hill. To reach this particular residence you have to climb countless steps as there is no access by car. Your arrival, however, is heralded by the encouraging, almost deafening chorus of crickets and the discordant barking of the resident Great Dane.

An oval, teak dining-table and high backed chairs (circa 1930), which are perfectly matched although purchased separately, set for a champagne lunch with brass goblets and contemporary plates. Partially in sight are two Art Deco prints by Sonia Delaunay and hanging by the arch is an English cast-iron oil lamp dating from the late 1800's.

29

Left : The open and simply furnished living-room. Shaded by the banana leaves is a group of four male figures, originally Sikh turban stands. Above, a portrait photograph on porcelain of an unknown Chinese man dating from the mid 1800's. On the floor is a wooden frog from Thailand containing a storage compartment. Both the antique chest and the clay hand-painted pot are Indonesian. The centre coffee-table is made up of two square low tables, inlaid with old English tiles and the conventional armchairs are brightened with modern printed ikats from Sumatra.

Top : Seated on an antique chaise-longue is a meditative, Indian wooden statue. Behind are two camel skin jars, used to store oil and water on long desert journeys, (presumably from India). A pair of fake, canvas, yucca trees from the Philippines prove highly effective in the decor.

Right : The entrance foyer with an original Art Deco wrought-iron and granite table. Purchased from a local junk shop, the origin of the solid, bronze dog is unknown. On the wall are a series of antique nautical prints and a Chinese wedding photograph of bygone days.

Left : An old Chinese rice barrel converted into a glass-topped table. The coarse woven mat on the floor is from Sarawak, it adds texture and variance to the predominant rich brown tones of the room. To further enhance the period of the house, Joseph installed the old fashioned tulip hanging lamps with counter weights, which were common features when the bungalow was built.

Below Left : The compact, narrow kitchen has *chengal* floor boards, which is unusual as kitchen floors were normally mosaic or tile in such houses. In the foreground is a set of English silver, dessert, stemmed cups. Also on the folding table is an old cast-iron and crystal candelabrum of European origin.

Below Right : An Indonesian clay pot on a stand hosts a spray of pink Nerines, framed by a pair of black and gold Chinese calligraphic panels.

The bed from the 1940's fitted with a mosquito net and a chair, believed to be from the same period, recreate with remarkable effect, the style and ambience of the colonial era in this guest bedroom. The batiks are traditional Javanese sarongs and the hanging redundant oar found in Indonesia now serves to decorate.

In a city of such diversity it would have been a shame to overlook this contemporary Japanese interior. The Davies family are part of the considerable, international, expatriate community and have already spent four years here. Previously, they lived in Moscow and Hong Kong, and although Mrs. Fumiko Davies has not lived in Japan since she left to study at the University of Moscow, her collection of Japanese furniture and objects keeps her in touch with her heritage and traditions.

The house is modern and semi-detached, with two further floors above the split-level dining and living-room area. The garden off the lower living-room is small, but provides a background of trees and greenery that, Fumiko points out, offers her the peace to paint or simply to watch the amazing variety of birds. Her stories include an encounter with a huge, colourful hornbill that used to visit and feast on bananas she would feed him by hand. He trusted her so much that he brought his daughter along - so Fumiko assured us - on several occasions. What a wonderful experience in a bustling city of skyscrapers and criss-crossing highways! On her overall impressions of Singapore, Fumiko adds: "It's great for family life".

The decor is a blend of the traditional and the contemporary, of the simplicity and purity of Japanese pieces and the intricacy of Chinese carvings. The floral designs are all meaningful, attributed to different Japanese schools of flower arrangement.

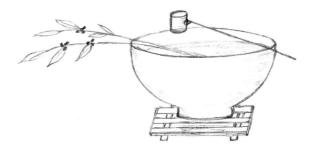

Japanese tea-ceremony corner tucked under the stairs in the main living-room. The accessories for the preparation of the tea are neatly placed on the *tatami* mats and by the step is a small *tsukubai* bowl used for hand washing before the rite. The painting is Chinese and depicts a country scene with a view that, in Chinese symbolism, is meant to bring happiness by its natural balance of the elements. Also hanging is a bamboo flute with a hook holding a teapot, which would have originally been placed over a pit fire. The fish acts as a lever and controls the length of the pole. The low piece beneath is a *hibachi,* meaning fire pot, made of wood lined with copper.

35

Above : A shot that includes an antique Japanese tea cabinet from the Kyoto area.

Top Right : A collection of Japanese masks. Among them is a *Hicosung* from an old temple which was used on special occasions (top left). The one with the long nose represents the demon spirit (top right), the white and gold mask represents a jester.

Middle Right : A pair of dolls, hand made by Fumiko's mother for her daughter.

Below Left : An intricately carved rosewood screen conceals the dining-room upstairs from the sitting-room below. The beautiful kimono on the balustrade was given to Fumiko when she was a child, part of a traditional Japanese celebration

held when a girl turns three. Children go through further initiations when they are five and seven. The heavy, antique, Japanese chest on wheels conceals many secret compartments as it was used by merchants to store money or documents. An old wooden pump occupies the corner and is signed by the person who made it.

(Previous page) Bottom right : The contemporary, western corner of the sitting-room. The coffee table is actually a low desk used by Japanese children taught in temples by monks.

Above : Fumiko studies the art of Japanese floral arrangement and the title of this lovely autumn composition translates into *"flowers left over from summer"*.

High in the sky, in one of the three apartment blocks of Draycott Towers, is the lively and urbane abode of Pierre and Chantal Gourragne. The French couple and their sons have much affection for Singapore having called it home for the last twenty years, making them almost 'Singaporeans' amongst the usually transient expatriate community. Pierre is in the shipping business and Chantal is the owner of *Beige and Blue*, a company selling decor items, many of which she designs.

Having previously lived in a colonial house, the Gourragnes moved to Draycott Towers six years ago. The circular blocks, a distinctive landmark at the time they were built in the seventies, stand a mere ten minute walk from Orchard Road, the shopping hub of the city. The principal room in this 2,500 square ft apartment, consists of a circular open plan living and dining area with the kitchen and utility quarters behind a swing door. The bedrooms are on a lower level which serves to separate them from the main floor. The decor consists, almost exclusively, of local articles and furnishings set against a backdrop of soaring skyscrapers seen through the encircling glass panelling.

Chantal has spent many hours exploring and searching through the more obscure corners of Singapore, from Chinatown to Little India. Rummaging in old stores, she has assembled a delightful array of local collectibles, porcelain, silverware, glassware and table linen, some of which will be highlighted in the following pages.

A blue and white sitting-room area decorated with an assortment of Chinese objects. On the glass and rattan coffee-table, a Chinese temple figurine in flight has been mounted on a Perspex stand. On the wall hangs a mirror from Thailand and a contemporary painting found in Malacca, Malaysia. In the foreground lies an antique Chinese carpet.

Above : In the background, an antique Chinese chest of drawers on which a celestial, Chinese, wooden statue sits solemnly, sheltered by a dramatic arrangement of papaya and banana leaves. In the foreground is a 1930's rattan armchair and a Chinese porcelain footstool.

Right : A view of the sitting-room as seen from the front entrance. Partly encircled by large glass windows covered with fine bamboo blinds to subdue the glare, it offers a staggering view of the city and the soaring skyscrapers. The monogram on the white chair cover adds a discreet, stylish touch.

Above : View from the sitting-room windows.

Left : The dining area which has been partially screened using the upper unit of an antique medicine cabinet, found in Chinese drugstores. Adorning the pillar are two graceful, Chinese portraits painted on glass and covering the windows are batik cloth blinds enhancing the colour scheme.

An alternative breakfast setting. On the wall, a striking, Vietnamese, hand-painted poster matches the vibrant colours of the quilted table-cloth from Provence, France. On the table is a set of cups and saucers with Queen Elizabeth II's initials (ER) used in the British Army's Officers Mess.

Cleared of the table (shown opposite page), the seating area returns to its usual arrangement. It is defined by a lowered, circular ceiling and the two steps down on either side lead to the immediate, adjoining bedrooms. On the original, colonial, rattan chairs have been placed lacquered, leather, Chinese pillows. An Indian oil painting hangs behind the high table upon which is a collection of antique decanters on a silver tray and a group of yellow Chinese ginger jars.

45

Left : A collection of old Chinese advertisement posters and among them a Singaporean marriage certificate dating from 1921.

Below left : The entrance passage furnished with a 1930's Chinese cabinet (of European influence) in bleached, teak wood. Three silver stemmed glass candleholders are placed together, the middle one decorated with a portrait of an Indian man, presumably commissioned. Next to them stands an Art Deco stem dish, similarly of European origin, and the antique painting, on glass, is of a floral composition from China.

Above : Chantal's fascination with the influence of symbolism in the quotidian lives of the Chinese has led her to collect, among other things, peaches in all materials and forms. In the foreground is a bunch of porcelain peaches, symbols of long life, in a stem dish. A collection of exquisite Chinese hairpins, some inlaid with Kingfisher feathers, stands out strikingly on the vivid pink table.

A Malacca Chinese kitchen cabinet, lined with a floral fabric, exhibits a collection of Chinese blue and white porcelain from the turn of the century. Below rests a Chinese symbolic, antique wooden carving and placed on the floor in a Perspex case is an array of precious, silk, hand-embroidered Nyonya (Straits Chinese) wedding slippers.

The master bedroom with a simple working table that holds a medley of personal papers and objects. An old Indonesian sarong hangs above the bed.

Sugar-cane, half a cabbage, a lotus and a spray of onion buds, held together by a long bean ribbon, make an artistic arrangement!

Robin and Monica Tomlin moved into this splendid colonial residence seven years ago, bringing with them some European antique furniture and heirlooms. A fair amount of renovation was done to the interior to restore some of the original features, even down to the old-fashioned bakelite door handles. Over the years, antiques and carpets from the region were added, placed to create an easy and inviting harmony. "I am very sensitive to the location of things in a room", says Monica. "There is a point, when furnishing, that a balance is struck and everything feels right. I look for this compatibility."

Although the residence is generously proportioned and could accommodate a great number of things, Monica Tomlin was careful not to crowd it so that the interesting architectural qualities and the personality of the house would not be overshadowed. Keeping the decor light and airy has been her objective.

The locations of the rooms are standard; the dining-room on the ground floor and the sitting or drawing-room on the first floor above the "carriage" porch. However, the asymmetrical position of the latter, which projects from one corner of the plan, differs from the conventional "three-bay across the front" colonial house. The perspective on entering the sitting room, is diamond shaped with an extended bay. Working around the tones in the carpets and kilims, the colours in the room remain warm and earthy and are counterpoised with white to offset the decorative items. The dining-room on the ground floor is just beyond the entrance hall and opens on to the terrace and garden through six adjacent pairs of French doors. To establish a definition over the doorways, Monica chose ruched batik drapes rather than curtains which she felt would interfere with the openness of the room.

Like many people living in Singapore, the Tomlins are fascinated by the variety of lifestyles and contrasts within this city state and think of it as "several worlds cohabiting".

Exterior shot of the impressive residence. Directly above the entrance porch is the upper floor sitting-room and terrace bay with its louvered windows overlooking the front garden. The jack-roof provides additional ventilation and light.

Top Left : The entrance foyer, furnished with a round table covered in a batik, and a German antique chest of drawers. Two large paintings grace the walls: an ancestral portrait and an oil and ink composition called *"Homage to Vivaldi"* by the Colombian painter, Rivera.

Left : One of the French doors in the dining-room defined by two panels of gold leaf pages from a Burmese prayer book mounted on Perspex.

Centre : The dining-room and, beyond the archway, another view of the foyer. The bust is of William Venables, sculptured in marble and dated 1840. Light coming through the open doors and the ventilation squares above them (now covered by glass) ensures that the room is always cheerful and bright on sunny days.

Top Right : The French doors open onto the surrounding verandah, overlooking the back garden and swimming pool.

Right : Side view of the residence.

Top : The extended bay of the upstairs sitting-room which accommodates two howdahs (a chair in which to sit on an elephant) placed together. Resting on the side-table is a clay pre-Columbian Maya parrot.

Below Left : Close-up of the glass-topped coffee-table on which is a collection of silver objects including antique English pieces.

Above : At the end of the corridor is a poster of a town party by Fernando Botero and a blue Italian pedestal vase holds a single Allium.

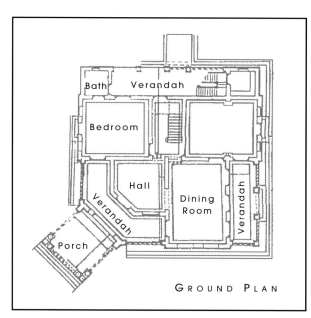

GROUND PLAN

Full view of the sitting-room. The geometric pattern of
the highly decorative Anatolia kilim draws attention.

Above : The master bedroom terrace with simple cane furniture. A lovely Javanese *sarong* serves as a table-cloth.

Left : The swimming pool.

The large master bedroom with a beautiful embroidered bedspread, hand made by Monica Tomlin's grandmother in Romania, an heirloom received as a wedding gift. The mirror-wardrobe is nineteenth century, of European design, but found in the Philippines.

Left and right : A romantic dinner setting under the stars. The low table is dressed with a heavy linen table-cloth from Romania and a tender arrangement of orchids and pink *"Lunette"* Anthurium in a highly polished, silver bowl.

Bruno and Soraya Stackler's home is a friendly oasis of oriental allure filled with the delightful laughter and activity of their five children. The Stacklers have lived in Asia for the past eleven years, drawn to the region by fascination and Soraya's Laotian origins. Their interior bears witness to their travels with an emphasis on Thai art and amongst the wall hangings are fine pieces of fabric and scarves, mainly European silks.

The 3,850 square ft apartment is in Arcadia Garden, designed in 1985 by the same architect who did the Singapore Shangri La's 'Garden Wing'. Featuring huge terraces which front the building, their apartment overlooks a canopy of mature trees providing a relaxing diversion from the confines of the rooms.

"Safe","efficient" and the "garden of Asia" seems to be the general consensus on Singapore to which Bruno adds "colourful". From the pastel facades of the old shophouses to the resplendent cascades of bougainvillaea, Singapore is certainly a kaleidoscopic urban landscape.

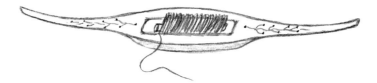

The sitting-room has a distinct Thai flavour, tastefully bringing together objets d'art and statues collected by the couple when they resided in Chiangmai (Thailand). Against the wall stand two 18th century figures, known as vestals, originally found at the entrance of Thai Buddhist temples. Hanging beside them is a textile from the other side of the world: a French woollen shawl used during the Battle of Austerlitz in 1804. Draped across the sofa is another exquisite shawl from the Italian king of paisley design, Ratti.

Left : Secured beside an old kitchen cabinet from China is a Siamese, ceremonial parasol and placed on a wooden bench is a bird cage in the form of a traditional Thai temple.

Below Left : A graceful Thai court figure stands beneath a spray of flowers and a distaff, still holding a yarn of silk, can be partially seen.

Right : A pair of antique Chinese doors forms the top of the dining-table and another pair separates the dining area from the family room.

The master bedroom includes a white cot for the new arrival in the family. Hanging above the baby's crib is a framed silk scarf, a gift from its creator, Louis Féraud.

A Thai showcase displays a collection of Indonesian, copper, stamping blocks used to print batik and a framed Valentino scarf bursts with colour. Somehow a little snail found his way into the long, low arrangement of orchids and lotus and slowly makes his way up to one of the Japanese bowls.

Singapore's conservation efforts have brought back to life many streets of old shophouses and semi-detached residential dwellings. One such terraced house is the venue of an art gallery, combined pied-à-terre. Built in the 1920's for a Chinese family, it was extensively restored to its former glory in 1988. Under the Conservation Act, alterations are restricted and the original exterior design of the building has to be faithfully adhered to. Although the architectural elements are European with the columns and wrought iron details, the central inner courtyard and simple grill windows are typical Chinese features. The two storey house is long and narrow with the bedrooms upstairs looking into the central atrium – locally referred to as an airwell. Originally open to rain or shine, the atrium has now been covered with a skylight which can be opened or closed as desired.

The downstairs gallery and lounge are elegantly and functionally combined to attend to client or guest. The white walls and floor and the clean lines of the contemporary furniture leave the space uncluttered and neutral for the paintings and sculptures on exhibition and the atrium allows the art to be viewed in natural light. The gallery represents many Singaporean and South East Asian artists, who, the owner believes, have now developed a language of their own. The distinction is apparent in their paintings through the quality of light, the unusual colour combinations and the perspective, which tends to be more two dimensional compared to European works.

Upstairs in the private apartment are the bedrooms, renovated to retain architectural integrity whilst providing modern comforts, such as a luxurious bathroom and built-in wardrobes. The master bedroom, the owner's favourite room, is intimate and very personal, filled with warmth and light filtered through fine blinds.

Previous page : The front of the house as seen from the street.

Top : Sunlight from the atrium brightens the long, narrow gallery and from her private apartment upstairs the owner can look down to see how things are going. In the foreground is *"River in the forest"*, a painting by Singaporean artist, Choy Moo Kheong.

Top : As you enter the gallery, a light and unobtrusive working table. On exhibition are two works by Singaporean painter Lim Kim Hai who chose the apple as the "leit-motif" of his art.

Right : A pair of comfortable sofas and a chrome chair share the gallery space and compose the main sitting and living area. On display is a collection of antique ceramics and pottery, including flasks and bowls from the Han, Liao and Tang Dynasties. The large painting is by Indian artist, Arakal.

The master bedroom, aesthetically simple and modest. A favourite room, the owner has only placed within it functional furniture and pieces of sentimental value.

The audacious colour schemes and the elegance of this inspiring interior are indications of an experienced hand. The creator of this decor is the interior designer of *"Studio 78"*, who chose to combine East and West by using a European basis - the furniture and window treatments for example - to highlight Buddhist statues and other Asian works of art.

This typical colonial "Mock Tudor" residence dates from 1938, and is built on a slope partially supported by stilts. The ground floor consists of a small foyer with a stairway. On the first floor are the sitting and dining-rooms with bedrooms arranged along a continuous verandah at the rear of the house. The interior has not been altered in any way, and the main floor still has the shuttered windows and the characteristic black and white blinds which provide relief from the strong sun. The original terrazzo floor has remained intact.

The sitting-room is a cool sanctuary with sponge-painted walls in purple hues and sofas and chairs in a soothing peach upholstery. In contrast to this is the vibrancy of the dining area, where the rich Eastern colours were inspired by the combinations of aqua, pink and yellow found in the Rajasthan palaces of India. The master and guest bedrooms are occidental in style, in pastel blue and pink respectively.

At the back of the house is a small brick-floored terrace covered by an awning lined with bamboo blinds. Cooled by a wall fan and the occasional breeze, it offers an alternative setting for meals amongst the lush palms in the company of the pet parrot.

The entrance stair-hall offers an impressive introduction to the eclectic interior beyond. Vying for attention, next to an English Regency chair and an acrylic on canvas by Arie Smit, is a Chinese, ceramic, Foo dog. The watercolour above the stairs is by Australian painter, Marianne Hay.

A partial view of the sitting-room as one comes up the stairs from the entrance hall and of the dining-room through the doorway. These rooms are richly and elegantly furnished with, amongst other things, a French 19th century tapestry; a wooden, standing, Burmese Buddha; two identical, ornate, Venetian mirrors.

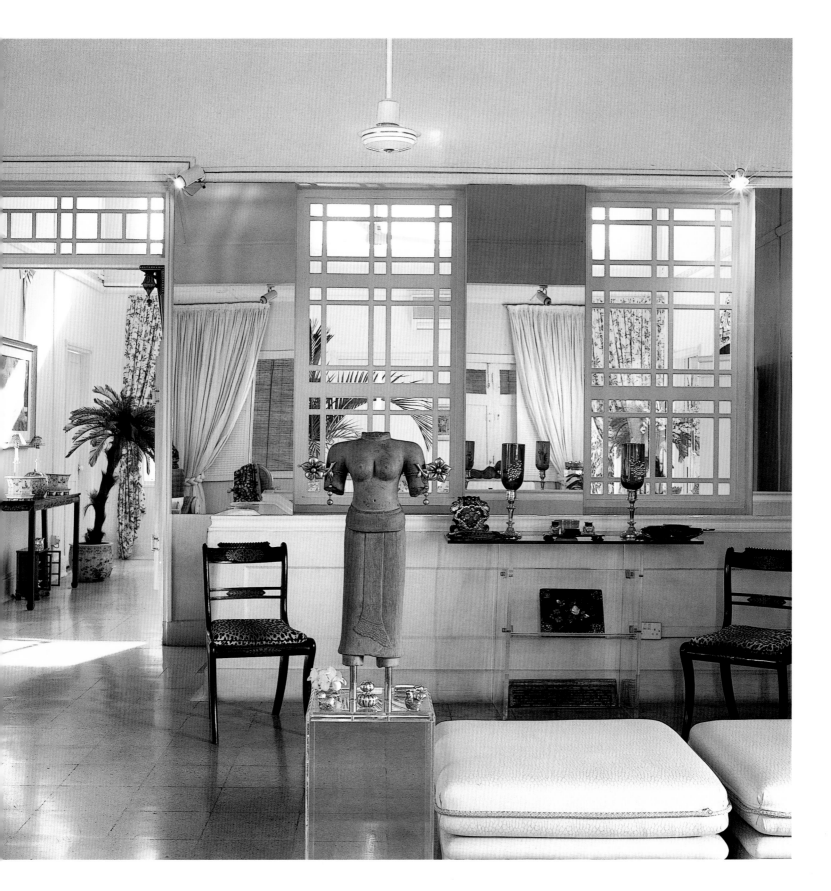

The chairs are Regency, inlaid with brass and the seats are covered with a leopard print. The stone torso is a Khmer piece and displayed on its Perspex stand is a collection of antique Cambodian silver. On the Perspex and glass side-table, stand a pair of turquoise, Venetian glass, storm lanterns with silver stems.

Top Left : A corner of the sitting-room furnished with a two-seater sofa and Perspex side-tables and stands, one displaying a wooden tray inlaid with mother of pearl and the other a gold and black Burmese lacquer box with an inscription dated 1937. Behind, is a bronze, reclining, Burmese

Centre : A full view of the sitting-room. A hand-woven *songket* from Kuantan, Malaysia, is draped on the sofa.

Left : In the background corner is a small, antique, Chinese altar.

Buddha presumably from the Mandalay period (19th century).

Top Right : A wooden Burmese Buddha from Pagan (presumably 16th-17th century) and a collection of red Burmese, lacquer boxes below. Set in a Perspex stand is a Chinese ceramic wash-bowl.

Right : An assortment of delicate objects : an antique Indonesian comb made of buffalo horn and gold; a golden Indonesian bangle; a bronze hand presumably from an ancient Thai statue; three animal-shaped Cambodian boxes and some Chinese porcelain pieces, including a cricket cage.

The master bedroom in blue and white with an English printed bedspread and matching wallpaper frieze. The seating area was originally a terrace which the present owners enclosed in order to enlarge the room.

Right : A Chinese embroidered hat probably used in opera.

Below : The guest bedroom in a soft, feminine combination of pink and blue, furnished with a wrought-iron, four poster bed, a pair of Regency chairs and a Georgian writing desk. Standing on the latter is an embroidered, Chinese collar piece.

77

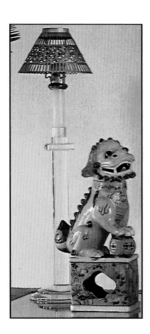

Top Left : A Chinese ceramic, *"Famille jaune"* Foo dog.

Top Right : An ornate, French antique mirror and a rattan and glass sideboard in the dining-room which displays some Chinese ceramic *"Famille jaune"* pieces from the late 1800's.

Left : A view of the dining-room. In one corner is a local display cabinet lined with a striking, printed fabric.

On the dining-room table is a pair of Regency storm lanterns on bronze pedestals and a contemporary, pink glass, fruit bowl. The standing Buddha is Burmese from Mandalay.

Above : The front of the house with a view of the swimming pool.

Left : A round table covered with a Chinese table-cloth encircled by chairs wrapped in white drill, create an alternative dining setting on the outdoor terrace.

A decorative iridescent shell on a stand makes a stunning container for flowers. Also, on the table, is a blue and white Chinese jar from the late Ching period, originally used to pickle ginger.

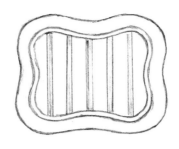

For the young couple, Chan Soo Khian, an architectural graduate from Yale, and his wife, Loretta, a graphic designer, this house was a lucky find. With their professional background, the task to renovate was an appealing venture and their approach was that of conservation adapted to today's lifestyle, rather than restoration. "We gutted the interior and started over again." The main concern, to bring in light and ventilation, was primarily resolved by adding a second air or light well in the principal room, in addition to the original airwell beyond the kitchen.

Antique carvings, acquired before the purchase of the house, were brought in and the proportions of the doorways and interior windows were built around them. Traditional Carrara marble was used for the ground floor and old salvaged floor boards for the two storeys above. An internal pond was added for evaporative cooling and the soothing sound of water which counteracts the noise of the busy street outside. Furnishings were chosen from the era when the house was built, such as the leather sofa and the dining-table by Le Corbusier.

Until the mid 1900's terrace houses like this one, built around 1928, dominated domestic architecture and were mostly inhabited by Chinese immigrants. They were initially simple timber dwellings but became more elaborate with the rise of the wealthy, Chinese, merchant families and their facades developed into an eclectic marriage of Chinese and European elements. Although the building forms were decreed by economics and also by council directives which required street fronts to be uniform, the basic principles and orientation of these houses were determined by tradition and geomancy. They were inward-looking, as family privacy was important, with rooms and spaces arranged around airwells or courtyards.

Right : The exterior of the house along the picturesque street. This flamboyant row and the one opposite are gazetted under the Conservation Act. Although mostly residential now, formerly many of the families living in them ran their businesses from the ground floor, hence the name "shophouses".

The main sitting-room furnished with a leather sofa by Le Corbusier (created in 1928, the same year as the house was built), a table designed by the owner and an armchair from the 1940's. The distinctive windows and the swing doors placed in front of the main door are original features of the house.

A pair of black velvet armchairs by Joseph Hoffman and a generous bouquet of Strelitzia and iris in a corner of the main hall are illuminated by a shaft of sunlight from the airwell.

Right : The indoor pond and beyond the embellished doorways, the dining-room. The kitchen and courtyard are through a further set of similar doorways.

Below : At the end of the indoor courtyard is a door which leads to a small, walled garden. Partially seen is the kitchen counter and on the wall is a window frame with shutters which has been cleverly converted into a mirror.

A table by Le Corbusier (1928) occupies the dining-room. The print on the wall is of the restored version of the Colosseum, by a group of French students from Ecole des Beaux Arts.

Left : The first floor corridor with bedrooms at both ends. The window that can be seen is in the guest bedroom and opens onto the airwell with a view of the main hall below. Although very modern in style, the chair by Mackintosh, at the end of the corridor, was designed in 1918.

Below : The doors and windows in the master bedroom were salvaged from old houses.

The plush bathroom, designed with a raised Jacuzzi bath and a separate shower.

Gracious living is an apt description of this cultured interior which reveals a sensibility of and passion for Asian art; each room in the house holds promise of further wonders and treasures. Travelling extensively throughout the region, as well as in South America, the owner has had many opportunities to delve and collect.

The residence, sitting on a slight hill and nestled in a mature garden, is peaceful and tranquil. Over the years it has been renovated and modified. To facilitate air-conditioning, the original louvered windows have been replaced with glass panes, the air vents have been sealed and the ceiling boarded. An additional room was built beneath the house and serves as a relaxing and cosy den, accommodating an intriguing collection of Indonesian and Polynesian artifacts.

The centre of the living-room is occupied by an exceptionally large, low, Thai table (6' by 9' 10") that was made to order using an opium mat as the top. Adorned by an assortment of interesting ornaments and books, it is occasionally cleared and surrounded by cushions when a Thai-style dinner is served. The formal dining-room is adjacent and the bedrooms, the master bedroom with an annexed study, are located on either side of the bungalow linked by a common corridor. The timber floor boards are intermittently alleviated by the luxuriant colours and intricate patterns of Persian and Afghan carpets and it seems that every corner and space has been attended to with thought and taste, composing an exotic and very oriental atmosphere.

The owner has an excellent impression of Singapore and Singaporeans. The well organised environment suits him well, even if some claim it is too restrictive, and he likens the city to a "gigantic garden".

A glorious gathering of blossoms in a Burmese lacquer offering bowl, surrounded by a silver swan, an English tea decanter and a wooden Burmese horseman and his steed.

Right : The sitting-room, in the evening, with the large, low, Thai table laid for a Thai dinner. In the spotlight is a standing Khmer stone statue, *Shiva Koa Ker*, dating from the 10th century. The antique, carved seats on each side are Chinese with hand painted details and the chest or *Tansu,* is Japanese. Persian carpets are scattered over the polished floor.

Above : At the top of the stairs a Japanese figure on an elephant, known as *Taishaku Ten,* holding in his hand an Indian police truncheon made of wood with a silver cap.

Right : The owner's two pet parrots, perched in a palm tree, enjoy a moment in the sun.

Below : The sitting-room captured in the morning light. On the coffee table, a variety of oriental and occidental ornaments and books share the space, including a blue French Art Nouveau dish from the Nancy school and an enamelled box created by the owner's grandfather, a renowned Art Deco artist.

Far Right : The splash of colours from the paintings add bright spots to this elegant dining-room. The Balinese painting is by Mewa-Pengosekam and the one in the impressionist manner is by Thai painter, Charoon Boonsuan. Surrounding the dining-table are Vietnamese coffee shop chairs inlaid with mother-of-pearl. Complementing the dinner service are decorative, silver Thai and Cambodian animals. Included in the crystalware are coloured, antique, Baccarat wine glasses.

Above : An Ecuadorian oil painting from the Quito school, dating from the 18th century. It represents St. Crispiniano and Saint Crispin, saints of cobblers.

Left: A spacious guest bedroom enriched by the warm and muted tones of the Afghan and Persian carpets. Above the bed are two mid-19th century English paintings of landscape scenes and an antique, Indonesian textile. On the bedside bench is an elephant tusk intricately carved with an African village story.

Above : A Japanese *Sendai* chest of drawers and an Indian mirror above which is an Ecuadorian painting dating from the 17th century by Samanego.

Top Left : A Korean feline painting presumably from the last century.

Top Centre: A Korean tiger painting of the same period.

Top Right : Looking out of the bedroom doorway.

Above : One of the guest bedrooms, just off the sitting-room, with twin beds covered in Thai silk. Above is a Japanese screen from the last century and the night-table beneath is Vietnamese, presumably from the Art Deco era. The other table is actually a Japanese tea box, ingeniously covered with a Thai fabric. The piece on it is a Chinese vanity case with a mirror. In the foreground is a Japanese lacquer table and standing serenely by the window is a Thai bronze Buddha from the early Ayudhya period.

Bottom Left : On the wall hang four antique Korean works of art. The chest of drawers is a Japanese *Kuruma Tantsu* from the Sendai area. On top of the two Japanese tea boxes are Burmese lacquer receptacles.

Top : Ivory holy heads from the Philippines.

Above : A modern showcase filled with compact discs upon which is a collection of Sukothai ceramics. On the wall is a work by Frenchman Jean Goulden entitled *"La Bretonne"*. Resting against the showcase, is an antique pipe probably from Nepal.

Above : A collection of family photographs add an intimate and private touch to the master bedroom. The soft tones of the Thai quilted bedspread work well with the colours in the carpets among which is a Chinese piece with a dragon motif. The nude oil study is by Filipino artist Malang and next to it is a painting representing a Balinese royal couple by Indonesian painter Anton. On the other side are two pencil drawings by the owner's grandfather and a pair of caricature pastels by Abel Févre, a pupil of Renoir.

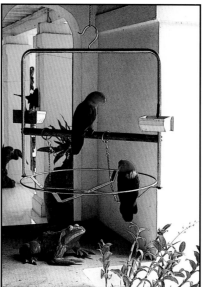

Extreme Left : A wooden ancestral statue from Atauro Lesser Sunda Island, Indonesia.

Top Left : The door of a Dayak house from Kalimantan.

Bottom Left : The owner's colourful pet parrots.

Below : An ancient, stone, horse head from Toraja, Indonesia on which is a carved bull and cockerel. It was presumably part of a tombstone. In the foreground is a Thai mythical animal, found in temples.

Right : A graceful wooden figure of a Balinese dancer.

Centre : A welcome in the entrance stair-hall by the statue of a Dayak woman.

103

Top Left : A fine *Gunungan* (bride) kneeling figure from Central Java. Behind is an Irian Jaya war shield.

Left : On the wall is a wooden shutter decorated with three faces and a bull from Sulawesi. The forbidding figure in front is from Papua New Guinea.

Centre : The enclosed den filled with fascinating primitive artifacts from Papua New Guinea, Indonesia and some of the surrounding secluded and mysterious islands. Large cushions, covered in Indian carpet, are casually scattered and leopard and tiger skins placed across the

floor further enhance the atmosphere of the room. Among the statues is a Sumatran Batak puppet draped in a robe (called a *Si Gale Gale*). These puppets were actually substitute "sons" used during the burial of a Toba man who had no male heir, as a man who died without a male descendant could only occupy a subordinate position in the land of the dead.

Top Right : A statue from Sulawesi, known as a *Toraja.*

Right : A Balinese carving representing a procession.

Far Left : View of the swimming pool.

Top Left : The driveway leading to the front porch.

Below Left : The front porch, now used as an outdoor seating area.

Above : A combination of orchids and banana and palm leaves makes an attractive tropical arrangement. Behind, framing the front doorway, are two Kalimantan ladders, used to climb up into the longhouses.

Books play a large part in the lives of Sharen and Mark Tan and access to the latest art and design books inspired Mark to approach the interior designing of his home and stores with an open and adventurous mind. Mark is the owner of *Page One,* the art and design book stores known for their specialty books, as well as for their distinctive shop interiors. When *Page One* was established in 1983, the aim was to provide material to support the creative needs of local artists, designers and photographers and, if they could not undertake international travel for inspiration, the books would bring the world to them. Plans for the future include publishing the work of local artists so that they may inspire others in return.

The couple engaged a Singaporean architect to assist them when they moved into this 2,000 square ft apartment. Walls were torn down to achieve spacious dimensions, floors were boarded with ingrained planks and ceiling features were added to create shapes and a flow throughout the interior. A curved wall was erected and spray-painted blue for effect and many of the features, such as the shutters and partition shelves, are mobile to allow for variation. The idea, Mark explains, is to take particular care with details so that the longer a visitor stays the more he or she discovers within this home. It should be more than just interior decorating, but also about encompassing and emphasising engineering and architectural aspects which require research and knowledge to achieve.

The modern, confident, black and blue sitting-room which combines wood, steel and glass, all elements present throughout the apartment. The curved wall contains tiny light bulbs which give the impression of elusive stars at night, these lights can be seen only at certain angles.

Top Left : A table and matching chairs of steel, wood, glass and Perspex were made to order for the dining-room.

Left : Two individual pieces make up this commissioned screen. It became a monumental process to bend the plywood layer by layer into shape, as the facilities to accomplish this by special machine were not available in Singapore.

Centre : A section of the principal room with a leather and steel armchair, a classic piece by Le Corbusier, and swing shelves which pivot around a fixed steel pole designed by the architect.

Top Right : The terrace where the family have most of their meals overlooks the rooftops of some old buildings on Mount Sofia.

Entering the shaded jungle road that leads to the property stirs a feeling of fascination. One might expect a wild animal to emerge from the shadows of the undergrowth, when, almost unexpectedly, one arrives in a vast, secluded clearing. Two large dogs charge upon approach, only to stop short, with tails wagging, to guide the way.

This house has an interesting history. It is situated in the north east of Singapore, surrounded by three or four acres of ground, part of the former Bukit Sembawang Rubber Estate. The estate was owned by two brothers, Lim Choong Pang and Lim Nee Soon, and covered almost a third of the island. The original house was built in 1909 and was used by the English manager of the plantation. During World War II it was badly damaged by shell fire and was left derelict until 1947 when it was rebuilt. Timber from the war-damaged Standard Chartered Bank in Battery Road was salvaged and used in the renovations. Much later, the estate and house were taken over by the government's Housing Development Board. Many tenants have come and gone, including an English lady who kept a horse in the garden and Chinese occupants who set up a joss stick factory, presumably illegal, for they were packed and gone one night.

The present owners are Frank Marciano and Robin Goh. Robin is an antique dealer who loves this island city and comments that she has seen many changes since her arrival in 1965: "When I first arrived, many areas were still large *kampongs.*"

The couple have an impressive collection of Asian artifacts and antiques, Frank being an enthusiastic collector and Robin keeping pieces she cannot bear to sell. The house offers the ideal setting for their treasures and a life in the manner they enjoy best; open and casual, hosting garden parties and living, one could say, a 1930's lifestyle in the 1990's. It is a sanctuary far from the "maddening crowd".

The only recent alteration, besides the addition of a swimming pool in the garden, was to enclose part of the terrace to create an extra room. As the house is so open - Robin explains - she has had to work with materials that can withstand the humidity. The floors are covered with coir matting from India made from coconut fibre, the wood furniture has been left natural and unfinished and the upholstery is confined to cottons for easy maintenance.

A composition of aboriginal artifacts including a wooden Batak statue of a mother and child and a Ming (circa 1650) farm cabinet from Taiwan, now filled with Indonesian sarongs.

Top Left : A view of the verandah from the garden.

Top Centre : A view of the house from the end of the driveway.

Top Right : A large tree with sprawling branches in the garden.

Below Right : A wooden Batak statue from Indonesia.

Below Left : The front verandah leading into the entrance passage. Resting on the ledge is a Balinese deer made from the trunk of a coconut tree. The contemporary, iron, folding chairs are from India and hanging are a basket wrapped in a sarong and two bird cages, one from the Philippines and the other from Sumba (off Bali).

Below Left : An old, wooden puppet from Sumatra called a *Si Gale Gale*. It is used as a substitute son during the burial rites when a Toba man dies without an heir.

Below Right : A food tray from Timor complete with a pulley. Originally, this was brought down in the daytime and left up at night. The round, flat disk at the top was to prevent rodents from reaching the dishes.

Left : Two Rajasthan (Indian state) chairs in wood and rope with iron fittings from the late 19th century. It is believed that these chairs were used by women in the courtyard as they did their daily chores. Next to one chair is a carved Koran stand and next to the other is an Indonesian betel nut box with all its accessories.

Below Left: The plaster and timber house stands in a three to four acre garden.

Left : A foursome of Gujarat (Indian state) statues stand on a sill looking out onto the garden.

Below Centre : A Mexican terracotta sun face, a garden bench and an antique Chinese tub make up one of many individual corners around the house.

Below Right : Part of the main verandah.

Top Left : A corner of the living-room decorated with an 18th century Burmese papier-mâché Buddha head, an Indian window from Rajasthan which has been converted into a mirror and a framed Indian tapestry which glitters as the light catches the pieces of cut glass that have been sewn on.

Bottom Left and centre : The open sitting-room furnished with an abundant variety of Eastern

antiques and, to bring the beautiful greenery closer, the doors have been mirrored to reflect the garden. In the foreground is a pair of Chinese elephant candlesticks originally placed on altar tables.

Above : A Southern Indian, painted, papier-mâché figure against a door panel from an old Malacca Chinese house (Malacca is a state in Malaysia).

Above : The dining-room, as with all the rooms in the house, is open to a splendid view of the garden. The local marble-top coffee shop table is set with English plates and green Mexican goblets.

Right : An antique, painted cabinet from a Sri Lankan temple; positioned on either side is a pair of blue and white flower stands. On the cabinet are Chinese lions, originally decorative features on shop sign-boards, and a Chinese silver soupier.

Centre : The passage which leads into the kitchen is furnished with a bamboo shelf displaying lacquer Chinese bowls, an old, English, chiming clock and two carvings holding a set of Chinese ladles.

Top : A papaya tree.

Below : A close up of the dining-table.

Left : A sporting Frank looks out the kitchen window for the photograph! In the courtyard an assortment of items and utensils: a bamboo chair from Taiwan, a Turkish wash basin, a brass jug and, against the wall, two long, wooden, Turkish bread moulds.

Top Left : A batik dyer's jar from Java, Indonesia.

Centre Left : A flower from the rare tree in the adjacent photograph.

Below Left : An arbour covered with creepers.

Top Right : A side aspect of the house.

Centre Right : A lotus flower.

Below Right : A wooden and cast-iron garden bench.

Above : Two cement benches and an Art Deco table under the shade of an Amherstia Nobilis, a rare flowering tree named after Lady Amherst, the wife of a former Governor of India. It was planted about 40 years ago by the last rubber planter of the estate to which the house once belonged . The hot day occasions the refreshment of a beer in this relaxing garden hideaway.

Beside a stained glass window, a rope bed with copper legs and posts from Northern India provides the perfect resting place for the pet cat, Fig. In the foreground, right, a small improvised low table displays a collection of old medicine bottles.

Top Centre : A Sri Lankan wooden, religious statue stands erect atop a Gujarat cabinet and a tall, Persian candlestick is partially seen.

Below Left : The guest bathroom with an exotic wallpaper depicting wild birds. To one side is an old Chinese wash stand. Above the modern basin is a tin mirror from Mexico and below are two Balinese ducks.

Below Right : An intricate Venetian mirror and an antique, Malacca Chinese side-table which Robin painted white. The smiling sitting Buddha is perceived as a symbol of prosperity and happiness.

Top : A wooden deck within the embrace of clusters of fine bamboo. At the edge of the deck, left, is a Balinese stone lantern and standing on a Chinese stone grinder is a blazing bouquet of yellow flowers from the surrounding jungle. Amongst the bamboo stems is a stone statue, called a *Ganesh,* from Bali and a smaller figure from Sumbawa (Indonesia).

Previous page, Bottom Left & Right : The bench table laid with late 19th century Nyonya (from Malaysia) porcelain and silver chopsticks. Silver chopsticks were often used by Chinese aristocracy as it was believed that the precious metal would tarnish if poison was in the food. The gilded, oil lamp stand is also Chinese.

Above : A wooden base for a grindstone from Rajasthan has been converted into this glass-topped table and features gathered pretty white flowers in a glass vase.

"A house on the roof " is how the owners describe their apartment in the Colonnade, a condominium designed by the American architect, Paul Rudolf. This spacious penthouse duplex is an interior decorator's dream. Proportions are luxurious and the double storey space, with the upper level gallery, allows for complete and uninterrupted openness. The sitting-room leads on to a terrace large enough to accommodate a cocktail party for fifty guests and offers the best bonus of high rise living - a panoramic view of the metropolis of Singapore.

The predominant choice of the appeasing apricot and salmon tones of the walls, carpeting and upholstery was to soften the space and establish an integrated base complemented by made-to-order furniture. Punctuating this composed and sophisticated interior 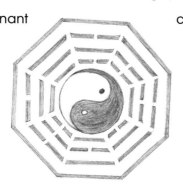 with vivacity is a golden, commissioned calligraphy by Tan Swie Hian, a Singaporean artist. Adding an oriental accent, the calligraphy sets off the other Asian pieces.

The imposing stairway leads to the first floor gallery and bedrooms and the sizable landing serves as an informal Thai-style sitting area. The master bedroom suite is wrapped in tones of pastel yellow and green. Fixed between two free-standing pillars are Burmese Buddhist manuscript leaves mounted on Perspex, serving as a headboard as well as a partition allowing the bed to be placed facing the view.

The interior design and detailing exerts a distinct influence on this decor which is mostly minimalist in ornamentation. In the entrance passage, carved Indian column ends make up the base of the glass-topped table. Twigs stretch out from a black, contemporary pot and flanking this centre-piece are two, wooden, Burmese Naga carvings.

Left : The principal sitting-room, above which is the encircling upper floor gallery. In the foreground, mounted like an abstract sculpture, is a wooden *Chofa,* a carving found on the roofs of Thai temples. In the centre of the antique Thai table (originally used as a day-bed) is a 15th century, Burmese, bronze Buddha with two rows of Burmese, carved bone, manuscript markers neatly arranged next to it. Behind the two seater sofa is a Chinese Han lady in clay, a piece believed to date from between 206 BC and AD 220.

On left wall : An impressive calligraphy by Tan Swie Hian. In his words: "The four Chinese characters are 啐啄同時 meaning to pick and to peck simultaneously. It is a Zen Koan: when an egg is hatched, the mother hen will pick at the shell from outside while the chick will peck from inside. The shell is then broken and new life sees light. Hence when duality is transcended, one reaches the source of creation."

Above : The Colonnade, considered one of the most exclusive condominiums in Singapore.

Above : The extensive, breezy terrace casually furnished with cane tables and chairs.

Right : The dining-room with a table custom-made to match the room's marble floor. Poised proudly in the middle are a pair of 17th century, Burmese, mythical lions known as *Chintehs,* and at both ends are two, silver, Christophe candelabra. In the foreground, on a high Perspex stand, a Chinese, clay, Han horse presides.

Left : Thai-style cushions make up the seating arrangement in this informal corner upstairs. On the wall is an Indonesian hand woven textile and propped up on the chest are two Indonesian *wayang kulit* shadow puppets made from goatskin.

Below Left : The bed and chaise-longue are strategically placed to optimise the impressive view of the city through the floor to ceiling windows.

Below Right : A soothing bouquet of apricot lilia, anthuria, white tulips and dainty paniculata.

Behind the bed in the master bedroom, a partition has been created
with Burmese manuscript leaves mounted on Perspex.

Moving around the fast paced city of Singapore you tend to forget that you are on a tropical island. Even the holiday-makers' itinerary usually involves frantic shopping for bargains in the abundant shops and boutiques and, as most of the residential developments and houses are away from the beaches and sea-front, the location of this residence is particularly unique and blissful. It was "love at first sight" for the de Saint Hilaires, although the house was uninhabitable as it had previously been stripped of bedrooms and kitchen to be converted into an office. The original lofty ceilings had been lowered, wall to wall carpeting hid the beautiful wooden floors upstairs and dirt the marble downstairs. Renovations took four months, but the challenge to revive this majestic old residence was a task Martine de Saint Hilaire took on with zeal.

The house was built in the early 1900's, presumably to lodge the Port Director, and is said to have later been used by the army's secret service (two years after moving in the children found a hidden, underground tunnel). It is approached by a semi-circular driveway that leads to a porch and is symmetrical in plan with three bays across the front. The rooms are of monumental proportions accentuated by high ceilings and exposed beams. Numerous arched doorways lead to inner suites and a centralised, Classical, detailed staircase in the grand entrance hall ascends to the first floor verandah which has a beautiful view out to sea. Evoking feelings of nostalgia, one can well imagine sunset cocktails and grand parties during the era of *stengahs* and long ball gowns.

For the de Saint Hilaires it is a way of experiencing two aspects of life, urban and provincial. Having lived in this region on and off since 1975, Martine concludes that Singapore is the cosiest place to reside in the Far East. " It's like a big garden, and although progress has changed the face of Singapore over the years, the people are clever enough to maintain some of their old traditions and preserve their heritage."

The open verandah on the first floor is used as the main living area. It overlooks the sea, busy with the passage of ferries, tug boats and the occasional yacht, and is favoured by a gentle breeze throughout the day. The furniture primarily consists of upholstered chairs with silk bolster pillows serving as arm rests, a low coffee-table, a carved Indonesian chest and the base of a Burmese lacquer offering box converted into a glass-topped side table. Amongst the ornaments on the coffee-table are a Vietnamese, ivory, opium pipe, a small antique chest from Cambodia inlaid with abalone shells, a wooden and wicker basket from Thailand and an old bowl used in the science of *feng-shui*.

Top Left : Seating occupies a corner of the vast ground floor hall and through the double doorway is a glimpse of another reception room.

Centre : The private driveway, announced by Traveller's Palms, winds its way up to the residence.

Left : One of two openings that lead to the dining-room. In the foreground is a Chinese celadon vase, acquired in Vietnam, and on the wall through the opening is a Korean chest and an antique Russian tapestry.

The marble hall receives visitors with a grand welcome. At the bottom of the centralised staircase is a pair of attendants bearing torches, thought to be commissioned pieces. Accompanying them on the steps are two red and gold Chinese lions and demanding equal attention is a large Chinese wooden horse.

The right side of the entrance hall as one enters the front door. Across the floor is a fine, antique Moroccan kilim and beneath a palm are two Balinese wooden deer, who seem to have been caught in a startled instant. At the end of the room is an antique Malacca Chinese (from Malaysia) cabinet placed against an Indonesian *ikat* fabric.

Although the 1930's, long, wooden dining-table can seat up to twenty people it has now been set for a tête-à-tête with two white peacock chairs. Dressing the table is an organza Spanish table-cloth, French Baccarat candlesticks, a pair of European gold plated vodka shots and small Vietnamese ceramic elephants carrying Chinese temple candles.

Top Left: A corner upstairs with a turn of the century Malacca Chinese (from Malaysia) desk and a Chinese antique chair. On the desk is an early 18th century Burmese Buddha with some of the owner's ceramic collection. The framed document on the wall is dated in the 19th century and has the signature and stamp of the penultimate Emperor of Vietnam. It records the presentation of gifts to a monastery.

Left : Part of the large verandah on the first floor serves as a delightful breakfast area. To one side is an antique Korean clothes chest and placed one on top of the other are two, red lacquer, Chinese chests. Sitting on them is a gilded, Vietnamese, lacquer Buddha.

Centre : The main area as one comes up the central staircase. Hanging from the ceiling is a golden dragon, originally found in Burmese temples and from which would normally hang a gong. On the wall are two, colourful, *Yao* (Northern Thai tribe) paintings on rice paper and between them is a mirrored window frame with lattice work, recommended by a Chinese geomancer to reflect the sea for good luck.

Top Right : The billiard room.

Right : The view of the pier from the billiard room.

Above : Sitting peacefully against a background of sky and sea is an 18th century Burmese papier-mâché Buddha.

Left : Another angle of the first floor verandah and its assortment of furnishings and carpets. The only relief and protection from the harsh mid-day sun and monsoon storms is provided by the black and white blinds.

A Korean *"trompe l'œil"* screen, a contemporary desk and armchair, a French 18th century child's chair and a Korean medicine cabinet decorate the master bedroom.

An arrangement of pink eustomas and lilies, protea, white orchids and palm leaves captured in a Cambodian lacquer bowl encrusted with glass pieces.

Perhaps overwhelming but undoubtedly impressive, this interior is contained within an elaborate web of exposed beams and wooden grids and includes a total view of the private, surrounding garden. The well tended flowering plants and trees, which attract a variety of birds, endow the interior with an animated peacefulness. When the Selvadurais purchased the land, after reassurances from an architect friend that it would not be too difficult to build on the tiered slope, Dr.Selvadurai knew only that she wanted a garden house which could be left open. The house was therefore constructed, eight years ago, with this in mind, incorporating several levels and numerous windows and glassed areas. The reason for the grids on the panes, the architect explained, was to give the illusion of many pictures seen through the individual squares.

Decorating began with the carpets which determined the colour scheme and a style was blended to suit the objets d'art and furnishings, most of which originate from India in particular, and South East Asia. The front doorway was widened to make way for a pair of carved, antique, teak doors which were found in Chettinad, India, following dogged inquiry and much perseverance. The effort was well worth it for they provide a fitting introduction to this home.

The garden shrine sheltering Ganesh, the Elephant God and 'remover of obstacles'.

The dining-table is laid out for an Indian-style dinner with brass goblets and plates lined with banana leaves. Above the mirrors hangs a long temple rubbing on rice paper from Angkor Wat (Cambodia).

Above : Through carved, Indian, antique doors a statue of Krishna beckons, poised with his flute, on a Thai table in the elegant entrance foyer.

Top Right : Along a passageway that leads from the entrance foyer to the outside terrace is an antique Chinese bench and table and at the end sits an Indian Goddess in bronze. A silk carpet from Kashmir lies across the cool marble floor.

Right : The terracotta finished tiles on the verandah provide a smooth, natural transition from the marble inside to the garden and are complemented by neat wooden and rattan chairs from Indonesia. The swing is an assembly of carvings put together to make the seat and a pair of antique brass chains taken from a Maharajah's palace in India.

Above : A Persian silk carpet depicting 'the tree of life' provides a luxurious background to an elementary arrangement of heliconia and leaves raised on a small brass stand.

Left : The interior, contained in a remarkable web of exposed beams and grids that allows an almost total view of the encircling garden.

"Nowhere in particular" is exactly where Bill Shepherd and Jim Bowen want to be when they come back to their apartment after a busy working day in the Lion City. That is to say, they chose to create an interior in a contemporary style that could belong anywhere and that does not constantly make them feel that they are in Singapore. Appointed with a blend of designer furniture and South East Asian antiques, American Arts and Craft artifacts and oriental items, this 1,600 square ft apartment suits them well. Two bedrooms have been converted into studies and a practical kitchen allows them to refine their culinary skills. The candid colour scheme came quite naturally, although the striking blue of the pillars proved quite a task to achieve. Three attempts later, and no compromise granted, the painter managed to come up with exactly the brilliance they wanted.

Speaking of their impressions of Singapore, Bill feels that during the course of the few years he has been here, it has become a more interesting habitat due to the conservation efforts, such as Boat Quay, and the increasing cultural and Arts promotions. Jim adds that Singapore is also a great springboard for travel around South East Asia.

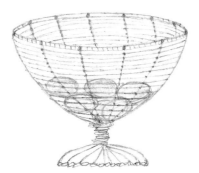

Bill's office furnished with a planter's chair from India, a copy of an American Arts & Craft desk made in Singapore in oak, book shelves containing some American Arts & Craft pieces and a basket pot from Lombok, Indonesia. An antique Balinese sarong and an African fabric are displayed on a stand. On the wall is a series of plans of South East Asian cities dating from around 1750.

A chrome Art Deco trolley provides refreshment in the sitting-room and a dark blue Andrée Putman carpet consolidates the candid colour scheme.

The dining and lounge areas are on different levels. Providing comfortable seating is an Australian armchair from the 1940's reupholstered in a Jim Thompson Thai silk. Above two Javanese chairs in wood and bamboo are Burmese temple panels depicting Buddha's life and resting against the wall on the upper level are painted wooden doors from Lombok, Indonesia. The dining-room features a mahogany and aluminum dining-table and matching chairs designed by Philip Starck.

Top : The polished marble bathroom.

Right : A stack of cartons makes an original makeshift wardrobe in the bedroom.

The well appointed kitchen with white and grey cabinetry and a central working table.

Karina Pellegrin describes her home as a love story. Her instant liking for the colonial house and the luxuriant, verdant surroundings inspired her to create a bright and cheerful interior. Selecting a floral fabric for the main room, she opted for a homely English country style to contrast with the exotic, romantic atmosphere of the spacious, wicker furnished, outdoor terrace. The family's favourite area is the sitting-room, the heart of the house, which is enriched with personal items that bring back memories of friends and countries visited.

Recent renovations refreshed the kitchen and bathrooms and air-conditioning was installed throughout the bungalow for extra comfort. A swimming pool and terrace were also added. Most of the furniture was bought in Singapore, while the paintings, chinaware, silver collection and other ornaments were collected during Philippe and Karina's previous postings to London, Hong Kong and the Middle East. Although the interior unites international elements, this very variety, combined with the architectural character and charm of these particular houses, suggests a style and ambience distinctive of Singapore.

Suspended from the archway between the dining and sitting-rooms is a pair of brass and glass lanterns from Syria. On a bamboo table is a trio of blue bottles holding stalks of ginger flowers.

Left : The airy and spacious sitting-room accommodates the plush, voluminous sofas well. These, together with the book-lined wall and view of the garden and swimming pool through the numerous windows, ensure that this room invites lingering, relaxing moments.

Centre : A Japanese 18th century box with embossed iris.

Right : Draped across the black lacquered coffee-table is a bright pink runner salvaged from the lining of an antique, Chinese, silk embroidery. A collection of English silver and crystal toiletry bottles and boxes is displayed.

Left and Right Page : The bleached wood table and chairs in the dining-room are from Malacca (Malaysia) and date from the 1940's. On the rattan console is a pair of English crystal decanters used on ships, hence the flat wide bottoms. The highlights of the room are two wooden model boats from Kenya displayed on Perspex stands. Freshly cut leaves placed inside distract attention from the stand itself, to give an illusion of boats floating in air.

Right : The colonial, timber, black and white bungalow raised on stilts.

Below : The attap-roofed patio overlooking the swimming pool and extensive garden, protected by seductive bamboo blinds from Thailand. The natural coloured wicker furniture combines with bamboo folding chairs; throw cushions in batik and plain silk add a stunning contrast. On the table is a cluster of frangipani and ginger flowers in a square lacquer box and straw mats are scattered on the floor.

Full view of the terrace with the breakfast table in the
foreground laid out for an intimate tête-à-tête.

A Chinese couple, painted on silk, preside over the master bedroom furnished with an Indonesian bench and a *Huanghuali* (type of wood) desk from China. In the corner is a Chinese, rosewood, reclining chair originally used to watch the moon - so the story goes.

A handmade wrought-iron candelabra from the Philippines
supports a cascade of frangipani fresh from the garden.

Chans Ville, the residence of Dr. and Mrs. Chan Ah Kow, was built around 1938. It is a fine example of a Tropical Art Deco house, a style which developed in the 1930's with the advent of new technology and the Modern Movement. The influence of the latter can be seen in the flat roof terrace and the horizontal, streamlined conformation. The house sits in a large, manicured garden with palm trees planted when the family first moved in. The ground floor has an open plan with no partitions between the entrance hall, living and dining-room.

Dr. Chan rented the residence in 1946 and eventually bought the property which included two adjoining pieces of land. The land was used to build tennis courts and during Dr.Chan's tenure as President of the Singapore Lawn Tennis Association many of the country's tennis players trained here. An enthusiastic sportsman and coach, he was awarded Coach of the Year three consecutive times, one of his many accomplishments. A truly illustrious family, the children were all active in sports as well; their success is evident in the countless trophies and medals on display.

The Chan's Art Deco villa. Parked under the porch is
Dr.Chan's sleek Jaguar E-type (1963).

On Text page : A web of branches laden with fruits from the Jambu Ayer tree that shades the porch.

Top Left : A row of Chinese garden stools and low palm trees.

Top Centre : A round display cabinet, a speciality craft of Korea.

Below Left : The residence is known as Chans Ville.

Below : The entrance hall, complemented by a splendid floral arrangement on an antique, marble-topped table from Indonesia. By the windows there is a pair of Chinese reclining chairs in rosewood.

Top Right : A front view of the residence from the garden.

Above : A shaded fish-pond filled with *Koi*, Japanese carp.

Top Left : Photographs taken by the children and paintings by Dr.Chan of family members are proudly displayed throughout the house.

Bottom Left : Partially seen are glass cases filled with countless sporting trophies and medals won by the family.

Centre : The sitting-room is comfortably furnished with Chesterfield leather sofas and armchairs, dominated by a portrait of Mrs.Chan painted by her husband.

Above : A Chinese antique, rosewood, display cabinet separates the entrance hall from the sitting-room.

The dining-room has more trophies and medals displayed. A centre-piece of garden flowers is held in a Chinese, amber, incense burner on the long, lace-covered table.

A grand floral display punctuated by tall stems of Heliconia.

Of all the old houses to have survived to this day, Inverturret, as the French Ambassador's Residence is called, is said to be one of the finest. Built in 1903, it was most likely designed by Regent Bidwell of Swan and Maclaren. Bidwell's most famous work is the Raffles Hotel, a renowned landmark in Singapore. Inverturret is considered unusual in the asymmetrical arrangement of the rooms, evidently positioned to take advantage of the best view. Square and compact in plan, among the obvious similarities it shares with earlier houses, however, are the broad encircling verandahs. The architectural

details and features are of exceptionally good quality and include thick, hand-made, glass window panes from Europe, rarely seen in old Singapore homes. Inverturret and Atbara, the bungalow housing the French Chancery, were bought by the Straits Trading Company in 1923 and have been rented to the French government since 1946 and 1939 respectively.

Monsieur and Madame de Montferrand spent over three years at Inverturret, personalising the interior with their impressive collection of modern paintings in particular. The decor of the "official areas" within a Residence, such as the main sitting and dining-rooms, is usually determined by a designer appointed by the Ministry of Foreign Affairs. The delightful yellow colour scheme, though, was chosen by Madame de Montferrand who feels that it is important for the family to live with colours they like, to feel comfortable and at home in a lifestyle that displaces them every three or four years.

By the window is a lithograph by Picasso, *"L'homme au Chat",* and resting
on the sill is a pair of porcelain birds from Germany and a Chinese jar.

Above : The residence, known as Inverturret. It is situated on an estate that includes the French Chancery next door.

Left : A lively profusion of orchids and lilies, and grasses.

The soft, yellow, sitting-room, seen through the Classical arches, is decorated with conventional seating and impressive modern paintings. The one in the foreground is *"La jeune fille á l'Eventail"* by Antonuicci.

Top Left : The painted staircase, located in a corner of the entrance hall.

Left : Straight ahead is the main entrance of the house seen through the arches from the sitting-room. To the side is another doorway which leads onto the encircling terrace.

Centre : Another angle of the sitting-room.

Top Right : Doorway that leads to an annex which projects from the side of the house.

Right : The enclosed, informally furnished, sunny annex along the verandah, reminiscent, in light and greenery, of a conservatory.

Above & Top Right : The dining-room, captivating in its simplicity and proportions.
Drawing attention is an abstract painting by Imais entitled *"Vogues d'hiver"*.

Below : A nosegay of matching white bougainvillaea placed in the napkins adds an attractive finishing touch to the table setting.

A fresh and inviting setting by the bay window.

Atbara, the building housing the French Chancery was built in 1898.
The bungalow is raised one floor in height and includes many unusual
architectural forms and details for a house from that period.

Decorating with ethnic fabrics and artifacts was the easiest way to work around this duplex apartment, explained the owners, a young Singaporean couple. They wanted the decor to be relaxed and flexible enabling them to add and move things occasionally. Balinese paintings, Native American pieces from Arizona and New Mexico, Chinese tables, a Nepalese 'tiger' rug and woven reed sofas from Thailand are some of the elements present. Clusters of green plants fill the corners and accents of colour radiate from the bright ethnic cushions. Artificial lighting is provided exclusively by strategically positioned ceiling spot lights.

Extensive renovations were done three years ago to update the interior of this apartment, situated in a low-rise building built in the 1970's. The alterations included a change throughout to 'white' Burmese teak floorboards and the front doorway, which was widened to insert large sliding doors. Only a central spiral staircase imposes upon the clean expanse of the ground floor area whilst windows remain unadorned except for fine bamboo blinds necessary to moderate the strong glare of the sun. At the far end of the room, an inset bench provides seating for the dining-table and small wall alcoves showcase various art pieces. Upstairs, the spacious landing is used as a library, lined with a thousand and one books and hundreds of miniature toys displayed on surrounding shelves. The guest bed-room features raised wooden platforms, a contemporary interpretation of the traditional Japanese style, and requires little flourish except for the comfort of a mattress. The luxurious monochrome bathroom is similarly on several levels, with steps leading to a raised bath designed to take advantage of the view.

Behind the sofa, in the background, the two large canvas paintings of bamboo affixed to the front sliding doors were commissioned from a Balinese artist.

Left : The sitting-room is casual and fashionable with comfortable low-lying sofas and chairs dotted with an assortment of colourful throw cushions. The two glass-topped coffee tables were originally baby cradles from India. An old Balinese batik painting hangs in the background and decorative plants fill the corners.

Top Right : A Chinese rosewood side-board, made up of seven triangular tables, provides a resting place for various ornaments, including an antique Thai bronze Buddha head and a beautiful old silver dish from Shanghai.

Below Right : A spiral staircase links the ground floor to the first floor bed-rooms and library.

Below : A pair of Balinese puppets.

A cushioned bench provides seating in the dining-room corner where the walls are fitted with alcoves highlighting individual pieces. The one above the bench holds a water-colour from Sedona, Arizona and another accommodates a small Navajo rug, also from Arizona.

A collection of *Kachina* dolls from an Indian reservation in
Arizona fill a few shelves of the book case and a Nepalese
tiger rug lies spread-eagled on the "white" teak floor.

Top Left : The all-white bathroom with a raised bath that permits a private view from the window.

Left : The spiral staircase leads directly into the centre of the library.

Centre : The multi-levels in the guest bedrooms provide the main feature and demand little furnishing or flourish.

Top Right : A quaint view over the roof tops of Emerald Hill.

Right : A spray of pale pink orchids combines with long stems of buds and bamboo in a fine Indonesian basket.

陳 瑞 獻 藝 術 館

TAN SWIE HIAN MUSEUM

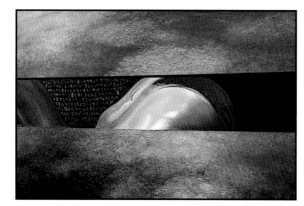

The creative world of Tan Swie Hian embraces his life as a painter, sculptor, calligrapher, author and poet. The versatility, originality, individuality and vitality that have long been evident in his creations are like many facets of a precious stone, so brilliant that one cannot gain a complete measure of them.

Tan Swie Hian was born in May 1943 in Indonesia. A Singapore citizen, he graduated in 1968 from the department of Modern Languages and Literature, Nanyang University. His publications include essays and fables, drawings and calligraphy. There have been numerous exhibitions from Tahiti to Taipei, in Paris and at home in Singapore.

Paintings, Clockwise from Far Left

The Bodhicitta Moves (1992)

Entering the Grassland to Spray the Wind

Gold Carp (1960)

Riding the Ox Home (1990)

Taming the Ox (1990)

Performances have attracted great kudos and he is the recipient of many decorations and awards. The Tan Swie Hian Museum features one who is living, yet has already made history. It records the true colours and spirit of the artist and poet - a perfect example is his monumental work that covers the entire museum floor.

The
REGENT

Featuring the atrium hotel design pioneered by American architect John Portman, the 441-room Regent is built around a very striking 14-storey atrium full of light and gracious lines.

The interior is marked by a blend of contemporary and traditional elements and the hotel today is renowned for one of the finest art and antique collections in Singapore.

The infinite attention to detail extends into the guest rooms and suites alike, where even the marble bathrooms are graced with regional objets d'art to evoke the feeling of an elegant private home.

Goodwood Park Hotel

On the 21st Sept 1900, a handsome building along the prestigious Scotts road was all set for the opening day. Music composed by Mozart and Bach filled the dance hall and exciting new electric lights blazed, bathing people and building in a festive glow. An anxious reception party was at hand to receive the most eminent of the five hundred invited guests - Sir Alexander Swettenham, Acting Governor of Singapore. This grand occasion was the opening of the German expatriate community's club, the Teutonia Club. And so began the history of the building now known as the Goodwood Park Hotel.

Situated on a gentle hill, the building was designed by one of the leading architects at the time, Regent Bidwell from Swan and Maclaren. The clubhouse was said to have cost St$20,000 and was a proud architectural manifestation inspired by the castles of the Rhine.

During the First World War, the British commandeered the clubhouse and it was not returned to the Germans. It was instead acquired by three brothers, the Manassehs, who initiated the building's revival. From an entertainment hall it became by the 1930's one of the best known hotels in Asia and in 1963 was purchased by its present owner, business tycoon Khoo Teck Puat. Having undergone extensions and periodic renovations to conserve its original features, it is today a 235 room award-wining hotel, the still imposing facade a reminder of its heritage.

The Goodwood Park Tower was declared a national monument in 1989 by Singapore's Preservation of Monuments Board.

THE

XTON

THE DUXTON

The Duxton Hotel is situated in the heart of Tanjong Pagar, in the vicinity of Chinatown. The site was originally a seven hectare nutmeg plantation owned by an Englishman named Mr. Duxton. The area began to develop much later than Chinatown and the shophouses here generally date from the 1890's to the 1940's. As was the prevalent style at the time, their facades express a charming eclectic mixture of Chinese, Malay and European elements.

Occupying several adjoining shophouses, the Duxton Hotel was opened in 1991, promoting "a home away from home" ambience and highly personalised service.

205

Alkaff Mansion

Alkaff Mansion, in its renovated splendour is an unusual entertainment and dining venue offering an enchanting dining experience - Rijstaffel. Reviving a colonial Dutch inspired tradition, an array of spicy Indonesian dishes are served at your table by a procession of ten lovely ladies.

The mansion was designed for grand living. It belonged to the Alkaffs, Arab immigrants, who had established themselves in Singapore as one of the most successful business families. Built in the early 1900's as their country home, the elevated site on Mount Faber Ridge commanded a spectacular view which was taken full advantage of by the design of the house.

The grounds covered a total of thirty-nine acres on two levels and featured manicured gardens planted with exotic trees and plants. The Sunday Times, on 16 Sept 1934, referred to the mansion as "a house which commands the finest situation in Singapore". The Alkaffs named the residence 'Mount Washington' and were renowned for hosting garden parties and lavish dinners, often receiving international as well as local dignitaries.

KINARA

North Indian Shore Cuisine

350-year-old Indian doors beckon you to explore the interior, where delights to the eye and palate await. Created with meticulous attention, Kinara brings to Singapore the atmosphere of a North Indian *haveli* or traditional bungalow.

The restaurant is situated on the popular café strip of Boat Quay, another of Singapore's many conservation projects.

Singapore
Palette

Favourite artifacts and personal collections from Cambodia or Bali, India, China, Thailand or Kalimantan all look at home, within these homes, against the spectacular backdrop that is Singapore. The city's environment is virtually spotless with beautifully tended verges, gracious trees, gardens and parks. The use of cars is tightly controlled; thus, despite the restricted land area, noxious traffic jams seldom irritate.

Restaurants cater for every taste, the chili crab is world famous and hawker stalls serve first-rate local dishes to thousands of patrons daily. Singapore offers a great choice from Italian, French and western cuisine to Indian, Japanese and many styles of Chinese cuisine - the immense emphasis on culinary excellence is renowned. Medical, educational, communication and transport facilities are first class, attracting foreigners and their families who find Singapore an ideal base.

Singaporeans are becoming increasingly sophisticated home owners. From renting Housing Development Board apartments they are now investing in a burgeoning property market, in a choice of brand new, state-of-the-art developments. Some of the architecture is particularly noteworthy, the finishing is usually of a high quality and the immense quantity of imported furnishings and fabrics lead to the consumer being spoilt for choice. The art of tastefully marrying the ingredients that make a gracious home is a challenge that can be enjoyed to the full. There are flea markets, shops selling everything from old phonograms to original cane designs from the Philippines, antiques from Penang and Malacca and warehouses stocking imported colonial antiques from former Dutch homes in Java or bungalows in India.

Home environments may be purely urban, or surrounded by abundant garden foliage, or, more rare despite being an island, overlooking a harbour or sea panorama. One can still see the occasional, highly prized, colonial home standing handsomely amidst well tended grounds. Interiors are minimalist or extravagant, traditional within a particular culture or a talented combination of old and new, east and west. Singaporean can mean originally Chinese, Straits Chinese, Malay, Eurasian, Indian, Armenian, European, - many different races have sought their fortune on this island and added their influences.

High Street was Singapore's first street, hacked out of the jungle in 1819 under the supervision of a Gunnery Officer from one of Raffles' escort ships. The Chinese community settled in streets set aside for the different dialect groups; Hokkien carpenters and merchants lived around Amoy Street and Telok Ayer Street, which, lined with shophouses, ran parallel to the coastline. Hainanese, known as excellent cooks, lived in Middle Road, Seah Street and Beach Road. The Arab-Malay community were to be found around Kampong Glam, the Malays at Katong and Geylang, Southern Indians at Serangoon.

Development expanded from what Raffles referred to as the Plain, now the Padang, which remains a prime venue for sports and ceremonial occasions. Reclamation work on the swampy south bank of the river led to Boat Quay and the centre for business and commerce was developed along the waterfront. Nutmeg plantations were established, the first rubber trees introduced and rural scenes were common until Singapore's growing population and post-war development, particularly since the 1970's, made drastic inroads and relentless construction and modernisation took over.

The river is no longer a bustling scene of water traffic but Keppel Harbour has expanded to a mammoth, super-efficient, container port. Oil tankers sail out onto their global chess board, cruise ships rotate their oriental voyages and tourists view the harbour from Chinese junks. New townships and industrial parks have spread the length and breadth of the island and the incredible choice of shops range from small family traders to leading department stores. Singapore thrives as a first class business centre, yet still retains historic aspects, traditional cultures and a unique and attractive style.

The Supreme Court, completed in 1939 on the site of the former Hotel de L'Europe, and I.M.Pei's outstanding architectural design of the Westin Stamford, the world's tallest hotel, part of the Raffles City complex.

Lines and Colours

1. C.K. Tang's and the pagoda-roofed hotel mark "the centre of town", once a rural area of fruit trees and nutmeg plantations. Tangs was founded in1934 by Tang Choon Keng who arrived in Singapore in 1923 from China. He sold Chinese wares in the residential districts first from a rickshaw, then from a bicycle.

2. Takashimaya, the largest of Singapore's many ultra-modern shopping complexes.

3. Singapore Cricket Club, established in 1852, in the foreground with the river, Boat Quay and the financial centre's skyscrapers behind. The modern giants seem to shield and enhance the graceful old buildings with their charm of the past.

4. Intricate architectural detail of Telok Ayer old market.

5. Reception hall of a modern office.

6. Chong Hua Tong Tou Teck Hwee Building, 853 Upper Serangoon Road. "A centre for Buddhists to pray, a truly spiritual building".

7. Ngee Ann City on Orchard Road is well entitled "city" with its two podium towers, huge choice of retail outlets, health club, night club and many other inviting facilities.

8. Decorated exterior archways of the railway station.

9. A glimpse of the port.

10. Boat Quay, once a thriving quayside crowded with boats and barges, is now a very popular restaurant venue for lunchtime and evening crowds.

11. *"Lau Pa Sat"* or Telok Ayer Market, now fully restored and offering a wide choice of food outlets. The market originally had access to the sea.

12. The distinctive columns of Raffles Place MRT Station, in the heart of the commercial district.

13. This glass frontage creates the maximum impact.

14, 15, 16. Housing Development Board apartments, like this one in Bedok, house some 87% of Singapore's population. They are meticulously kept, with community facilities, markets, hawker food stalls and small parks close by. They are often linked from one side of the road to the other by overhead bridges overflowing with colourful bougainvillaea.

17. A corner of Koon Seng Road.

18. Lovely old windows of Jalan Madras in Little India.

19. A quiet street of charming shophouses.

21. Gat House, formerly home to German Asian Travel, it has now been renovated and resurrected in green and white!

22. A fruit stall displaying different varieties of banana.

20. 379 Upper Paya Lebar Road houses "Just Anthony". Here customers can find a great choice of Chinese antiquities plus French pieces from Vietnam. An Australian collector subsequently bought the beautiful Chinese wedding cart pictured, it was originally used to transport the bride to her wedding.

23. God Festival in Lorong Telok.

24, 25. Thian Hok Keng Temple, the most important Hokkien temple and a Singapore showpiece. A shrine was first erected on this site at the time of the foundation of Singapore in 1819, dedicated to the Goddess of the Sea.

26. Thian Hok Keng Temple was completed in 1840. The two Door Gods guard the entrance and throughout the temple there is much elaborate detail.

27. Flower sellers outside the Kwan Im Thong Hood Cho Temple in Waterloo Street, a temple popular for "praying, requesting predictions and receiving advice". One of the small altars is dedicated to a famous doctor of the Han dynasty, a patron saint of Chinese medicine.

28, 29. Tan Si Chong Su Temple, Magazine Road, is the ancestral temple of the Tan clan. It was built in 1876. mainly at the expense of Tan Kim Ching and Tan Beng Swee, the wealthy sons of the pioneer and philanthropist Tan Tock Seng and Tan Kim Seng respectively. This temple used to stand among the godowns on the bank of the river. The scene has completely changed; however the temple remains, gazetted for conservation.

30. Fu Tak Ch'i temple. First established in 1820, It was one of the earliest temples in Singapore dedicated to Toh Peh Kong and was patronised by Cantonese and Hakkas. This temple was sadly marked for closure in mid-1994 and some of the artifacts were passed to the Singapore History Museum.

31, 32, 33. The Wak Hai Cheng Bio Temple in Philip Street, with its large open courtyard which once stood near the seashore belies the fact that it is now completely overlooked by towering city skyscrapers. It is a Teochew temple dating from the 1820s, rebuilt in 1852-1855. Soon after, it became the asset of the Ngee Ann Company. This temple is full of vitality, there are legendary pictures engraved on the temple walls, porcelain figures all over the roof and long life joss sticks strung across the courtyard.

34. A lone member of the audience in the Singapore Federation of Chinese Clan Associations.

35. Sri Krishnan Temple, Waterloo Street. Mr Hanuman Beem Singh found a Banyan tree in an open field, cleared the ground and placed the deities of Sri Vigneshwarar and Sri Hanuman at the foot of the tree. Eventually he built an attap hut for Lord Krishna. The new temple was completed in 1959.

38, 39, 40. Madras Palyakat Trading, sarong importers and exporters at 241 Beach Road. Head office Madras, branches Singapore and Penang.

41. The Sultan Mosque, the first mosque on this site, was built in 1824. The grandson of Sultan Hussein, the signatory to Raffles' first treaty in 1819, Sultan Ali (1835-1877), known as Sultan of the Faithful, is buried in the precincts.

36. Jasmine garland stall

37. Durgha Shrine beside Telok Ayer Green was built by South Indian Muslims between 1828 and 1830 in memory of Shahul Hamid, a pious Muslim.

42. These beautiful, decorative tiles were commonly used to grace the facades of many shops and homes.

43. The corner of Arab Street - everybody's favourite rattan shop.

Passengers waiting inside the railway station are overlooked by six magnificent mosaics, each in three panels, of rural and harbour scenes.

The first section of railway in Singapore was opened in 1903; by 1923 passenger trains were able to cross the Causeway to Johor and in 1932 the Railway Station to Keppel Road was completed. The Central Waiting Hall has a dome roof, the walls are panelled with typical Malaysian scenes and the Habib Railway Book Store continues to operate as it has done since 1936. Outside, Art Deco lines combine with a Chinese-style roof. Four white statues represent Agriculture, Commerce, Transport and Industry and The Federated Malay States Railway displays an appropriate banner "Welcome to Malaysia". The peninsula beckons as commuter, express, daily mail trains set off north from Platform 2, towards the kampongs and plantations, forest and rice fields of Malaysia and on to Thailand. The magnificent Eastern & Oriental Express also runs from here.

The End of The Journey
Wednesday 20th October 1993, 11.20 am.

Nicoline's most important equipment
used during the photography

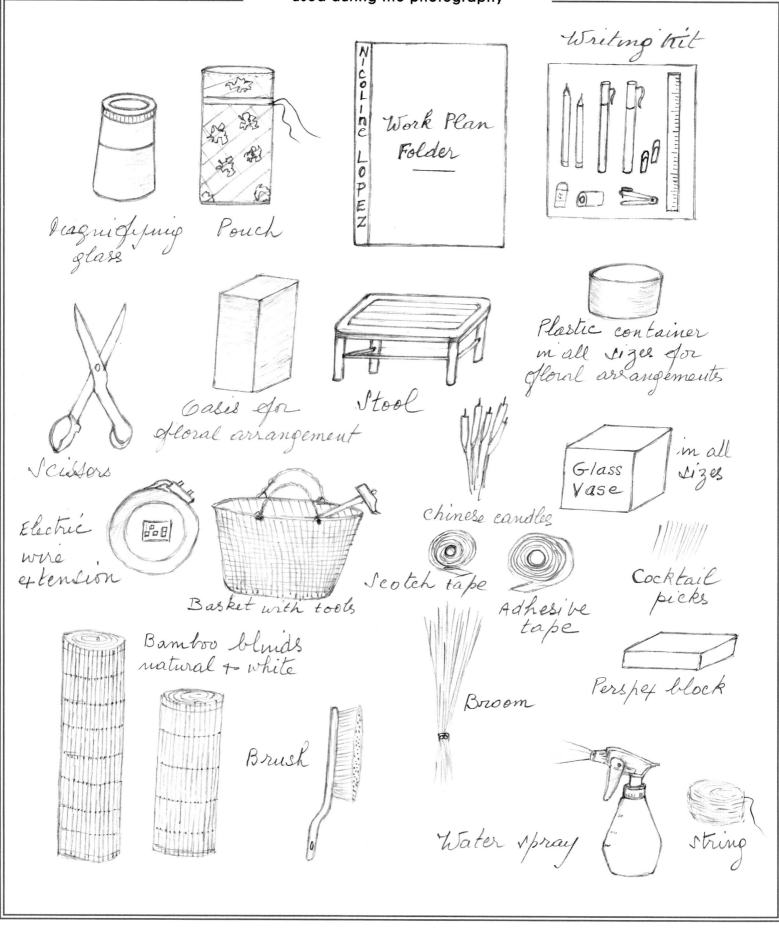

Magnifying glass

Pouch

NICOLINE LOPEZ
Work Plan Folder

Writing kit

Scissors

Oasis for floral arrangement

Stool

Plastic container in all sizes for floral arrangements

Glass Vase

in all sizes

Electric wire extension

Basket with tools

chinese candles

Scotch tape

Adhesive tape

Cocktail picks

Bamboo blinds natural + white

Brush

Broom

Perspex block

Water spray

string

SINGAPORE

1 Singapore Crocodilarium
2 Singapore Crocodile Farm
3 Haw Par Villa
4 Ming Village
5 Singapore Science Centre
6 Chinese Garden
7 Japanese Garden
8 Jurong Crocodile Paradise
9 Jurong Bird Park
10 Bukit Turf Club
11 Bukit Timah Nature Reserve
12 Singapore Zoological Gardens
13 Mandai Orchid Garden
14 Changi Airport
15 Sentosa
16 Causeway

A Chinatown
B Orchard District
C Little India
D Colonial District
E Arab Street

A CHINATOWN

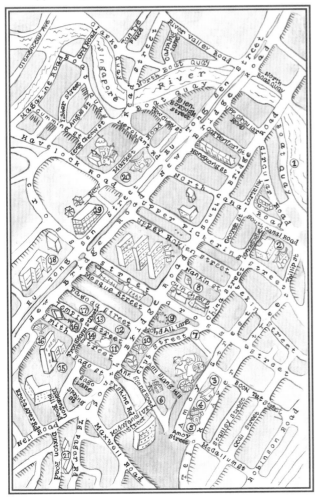

1 Boat Quay
2 Wak Hai Cheng Bio Temple
3 Nagore Durgha Shrine
4 Thian Hock Keng Temple
5 Al-Abrar Mosque
6 Noodle Restaurant
7 Temple Idol Carvers
8 Chinese Tea Shop
9 Goldsmiths
10 Masks, Lion Dance Heads
11 Temple, Shops, Tinsmiths
12 Sri Mariaman Temple
13 Dried Mushrooms
14 Porcelain Housewares
15 Chinatown Complex
16 Kites, Fans
17 Dishes, Clogs
18 People's Park Shopping Complex
19 People's Park Centre
20 Thong Chai Medical Inst
21 Tanjong Pagar Conservation Area

B ORCHARD DISTRICT

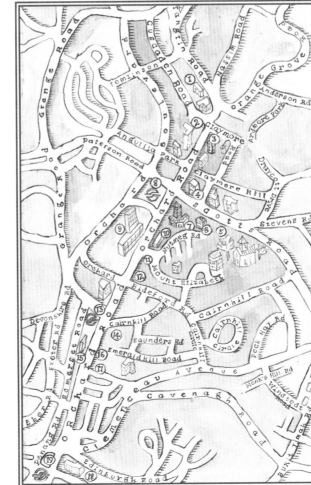

1 Tanglin Shopping Centre
2 Forum Galleria
3 Orchard Towers
4 Shaw Centre
5 Far East Plaza
6 Scotts Shopping Centre
7 Tangs
8 Orchard MRT Station
9 Wisma Atria
10 Lucky Plaza
11 The Promenade
12 Paragon Shopping Centre
13 Somerset MRT Station
14 OG Building
15 Specialists' Centre
16 Peranakan Place
17 Centrepoint
18 Plaza Singapura
19 Dhoby Ghaut MRT Station

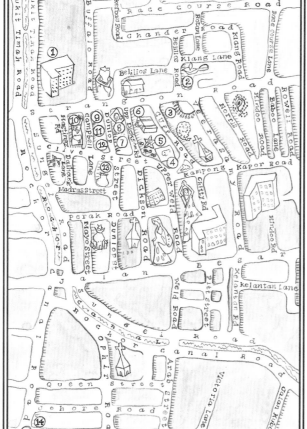

1 Zhu Jiao Market

2 Sri Veeramakaliaman Temple

3 Goldsmiths

4 Fish Head Curry

5 Spice & Lentil Mill

6 Luggage, Trunks

7 Komala Vilas Vegetarian Restaurant

8 Poster Seller

9 Spices & Dry Goods

10 Sari Shops

11 Garlands

12 Provision Shops

13 Traditional Kitchen Utensils

14 Bugis MRT Station

D COLONIAL DISTRICT

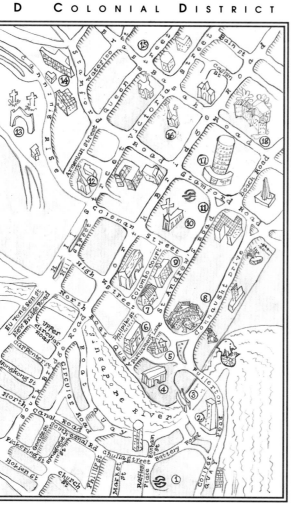

1 Raffles Place MRT Station

2 Fullerton Bldg

3 Cavenagh Bridge

4 The Empress Place

5 Victoria Concert Hall & Theatre

6 Parliament House

7 Supreme Court

8 Singapore Cricket Club

9 City Hall

10 St Andrew's Cathedral

11 City Hall MRT Station

12 Armenian Church

13 Fort Canning Park

14 National Museum & Art Gallery

15 St Joseph's Institution Building

16 Convent of the Holy Infant Jesus

17 Raffles City

18 Raffles Hotel

E ARAB STREET

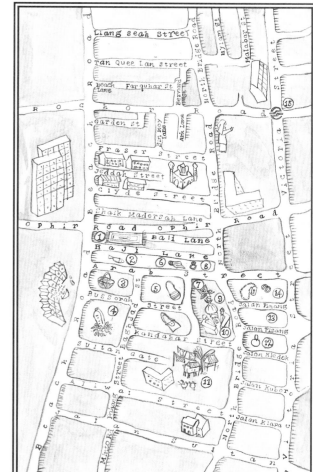

1 Textiles

2 Fishing Tackle

3 Cane & Basketware

4 Muslim Gravestone Makers

5 Indian, Leather Sandals & Bags

6 Batik, Textiles, Clothing

7 Indian Herbs & Spices

8 Jewellers

9 Prata Makers

10 Sultan Mosque

11 Istana Kampong Glam

12 Perfume Essences

13 Dancers' & Brides' Jewellery & Accessories

14 Goldsmiths

15 Bugis MRT Station

The Art **of** Shopping

Superb antique Thai Buddha head
from the collection of

La Dame de Malacca

ANTIQUES

MATA-HARI
Arts & Antiques of S.E. Asia

#02-26
Tanglin Shopping Centre,
19, Tanglin Road,
Singapore 1024
Tel : (65) 737 6068
Fax : (65) 738 3579

*Collections of antique
silverware and gold jewelry.
Artifacts from the Golden
Triangle. Bronze and wooden
Buddhas. Old Laotian and
Cambodian textiles.*

Window to the past

60B, Martin Road
#04-06, Trademart (S) Pte Ltd
Singapore 0923

Tel : (65) 235 2760
Fax : (65) 734 3327

*Genuine 19th & 20th century
Colonial furniture and exotic
craft of Asia*

ART GALLERIES

ART FOCUS GALLERY

176 Orchard Road #05-07,
Centrepoint,
Singapore 0923

Tel : (65) 733 8337

*Original artworks, limited
edition prints &
framing services*

Four Seasons Hotel Singapore

Tel : (65) 734 2070
Fax : (65) 735 7006

Fine Contemporary Works of Art

ANTIQUES

La Dame de Malacca
Nicoline Lopez
20A, Jalan Mamanda 5, Ampang Point,
68000 Selangor, Malaysia
Tel : (603) 451 1308   Fax : (603) 451 7079
Fine Thai and Burmese antiques.

TERESA COLEMAN FINE ARTS LTD

37, Wyndham Street
Central, Hong Kong
Tel : (852) 526 2450

*Antique Chinese Textiles, Fans,
Paintings, Rugs and Tibetan Artifacts*

TEMPO DOELOE ETHNIC ARTS

Raffles Hotel Arcade
328 North Bridge Road
#02-33 Singapore 0718
Tel : (65) 338 1036

Buddhas, Textiles & Lacquerware

JUST ANTHONY

379, Upper Paya Lebar Road, Singapore 1953
Tel : (65) 283 4782, 283 4722   Fax : 284 7439

Antique Importers and Exporters

 **TIEPOLO PREMIER ANTIQUES**

#02-23 Tanglin Shopping Centre,
19, Tanglin Road, Singapore 1024
Tel : (65) 732 7924   Fax : (65) 732 7279

Asian antiques

ART GALLERIES

Shenn's Fine Art

8, Bukit Pasoh Road
(off Neil Road)
Singapore 0208

Tel : (65) 223 1233
Fax : (65) 223 1238

*Dealer in contemporary local &
South East Asian Fine Art.*

SHENN'S FINE ART

Private viewing Sat: at 37, Blair Rd by appointment only

First French Art Gallery
Orchard Hotel Shopping Arcade, 442 Orchard Road, Singapore 0923
Tel : (65) 735 2618   /   Fax : (65) 735 2616
Contemporary & 19th Century Paintings

ANTIQUES

ROBIN GOH
Director

31A - 33A, Cuppage Terrace
Singapore 0923

Tel : (65) 235 7866

Fax : (65) 734 8665

*Indian antiques, architectural
pieces & home furnishings*

EASTERN DREAMS SDN. BHD.
Hotel Equatorial
Lot 17, Mid-Level Floor,
Jalan Sultan Ismail
50250 Kuala Lumpur, Malaysia
Tel : (603) 263 4248
Fax : (603) 263 4249

Antiques & Fine Arts

ANTIQUE SILVER PTE. LTD.
Esmé Parish
Tel : (65) 735 1180
Fax : (65) 735 1186
*Superb Chinese Export &
English Silver. Modern Picture
Frames & Other Gift Items*

ART GALLERIES

PLUM BLOSSOMS GALLERY
#02-37 Raffles Hotel Arcade
Singapore 0718
Tel : (65) 334 1198

305 - 307 Exchange Square One
Hong Kong

*Contemporary Asian Painting,
Antique Textiles, Tibetan
Carpets and Artifacts*